CRACKING Writing

Teacher's Guide

Kate Ruttle

RISING STARS

YEAR 6

Hachette UK's policy is to use papers that are natural, renewable and recyclable products and made from wood grown in sustainable forests. The logging and manufacturing processes are expected to conform to the environmental regulations of the country of origin.

Orders: please contact Bookpoint Ltd, 130 Park Drive, Milton Park, Abingdon, Oxon OX14 4SE. Telephone: (44) 01235 400555.
Email primary@bookpoint.co.uk

Lines are open from 9 a.m. to 5 p.m., Monday to Saturday, with a 24-hour message answering service. Visit our website at www.risingstars-uk.com for details of the full range of Rising Stars publications.
Online support and queries:
Email: onlinesupport@risingstars-uk.com

ISBN: 978-1-51040-202-7

Text, design and layout © 2017 Rising Stars UK Ltd
First published in 2017 by Rising Stars UK Ltd
Rising Stars UK Ltd, part of Hodder Education Group
An Hachette UK Company
Carmelite House, 50 Victoria Embankment, London EC4Y 0DZ
www.risingstars-uk.com
Impression number 10 9 8 7 6 5 4 3 2 1
Year   2020 2019 2018 2017

All rights reserved. Apart from any use permitted under UK copyright law, the material in this publication is copyright and cannot be photocopied or otherwise produced in its entirety or copied onto acetate without permission. Electronic copying is not permitted. Permission is given to teachers to make copies of individual pages marked © Rising Stars UK Ltd, for classroom distribution only, to pupils within their own school or educational institution. The material may not be copied in unlimited quantities, kept on behalf of others, distributed outside the purchasing institution, copied onwards, sold to third parties, or stored for future use in a retrieval system. This permission is subject to the payment of the purchase price of the book. If you wish to use the material in any way other than as specified you must apply in writing to the Publisher at the above address.

Author: Kate Ruttle
Publishers: Laura White and Nick Hunter
Illustrator: Clair Rossiter, Bright Group International
Text design, logo and cover design: Julie Martin
Typesetting: Aptara Inc.
Copy Editor: Lesley Densham
Proofreader: Debbie Allen
Project editor: Rachel Nickolds
Printed in United Kingdom by Ashford Colour Press Ltd.

A catalogue record for this title is available from the British Library.

Acknowledgements

Every effort has been made to trace all copyright holders, but if any have been inadvertently overlooked, the Publishers will be pleased to make the necessary arrangements at the first opportunity.

Although every effort has been made to ensure that website addresses are correct at time of going to press, Rising Stars cannot be held responsible for the content of any website mentioned in this book. It is sometimes possible to find a relocated web page by typing in the address of the home page for a website in the URL window of your browser.

The Publishers would like to thank the following for permission to reproduce copyright material.

Text acknowledgements

p6 from *My Family and Other Animals* by Gerald Durrell; p17 from *Moon Bear* by Gill Lewis; p27 *A Wrinkle in Time* by Madeleine L'Engle; from *Macbeth* by William Shakespeare, retold and illustrated by Marcia Williams. Copyright © 2015 Marcia Williams, reproduced by permission of Walker Books Ltd, London SE11 5HJ www.walker.co.uk; p49 'Ancient and Medieval Art' from *The Usborne Introduction to Art* by Rosie Dickens, published by Usborne Publishing Limited; p60 from *Bullies, Bigmouths and So-Called Friends* by Jenny Alexander published by Hodder Children's Books; p71 from *The Vanishing Rainforest* by Richard Platt; p95 'What is the World?' by James Carter from *Is This a Poem?* edited by Roger Stevens © Jame s Carter by permission of Bloomsbury Publishing Plc.

Photo acknowledgements

p49 Everett Historical/Shutterstock; p50 ColoArt/Shutterstock; p83 Iurii Osadchi/Shutterstock; p84 Gianni Caito/Shutterstock.

Contents

Unit	Focus for writing	Text	Text analysis includes:	Page
Fiction				
1	Using dialogue to clarify relationships and advance plot	extract from **My Family and Other Animals** by Gerald Durrell	*content*: characters, plot development *structure*: dialogue, punctuation, vocabulary	6
2	Developing a story within its setting	extract from **Moon Bear** by Gill Lewis	*content*: setting, plot development *structure*: paragraphs, cohesion, vocabulary, sentence length	17
3	Writing a science fiction/fantasy story	*Into the Future* A retelling of **The Time Machine** by H. G. Wells	*content*: setting, plot development *structure*: paragraphs, cohesion, vocabulary, sentence length (including passives)	27
4	Retelling part of a story	extract from **Macbeth** retold by Marcia Williams	*content*: characters, plot development *structure*: language (including passives and modal verbs), cohesion, vocabulary	38
Non-fiction				
5	Writing a formal information text	'Ancient and Medieval Art' from *The Usborne Introduction to Art* by Rosie Dickens	*structure and organisation*: headings, organisation and progression of ideas, paragraphs *purpose and language*: formal language and sentence structure, punctuation	49
6	Writing an informal information and procedural text (instructions)	extract from **Bullies, Bigmouths and So-Called Friends** by Jenny Alexander	*structure and organisation*: headings and organisation, structure, topic sentences *purpose and language*: purpose, comparing language for different purposes, informal language	60
7	Writing a biased text and story with the same message	extract from **The Vanishing Rainforest** by Richard Platt	*structure and organisation*: comparing features of fiction and persuasive texts *purpose and language*: identifying persuasive techniques, comparing language and vocabulary, punctuation	71
8	Writing a discussion	**Where Should Sports Funding Be Aimed?**	*structure and organisation*: summarising, progression of ideas, paragraphs *purpose and language*: cohesion, adverbials, prepositions and conjunctions, formality, punctuation	83
Poetry				
9	Writing free verse	**What is the World?** by James Carter	*content*: mood, vocabulary, idea development *structure*: rhythm and rhyme, punctuation	94

Introduction

What is *Cracking Writing*?

Cracking Writing is a step-by-step resource to improve children's composition and writing skills. The advice and guidance in this *Teacher's Guide* will help you to teach children the skills and strategies they need to write effectively for a wide range of purposes. The approach combines creativity and intention with a thorough understanding of grammar in context, and will enable you to successfully deliver the expectations of the 2014 National Curriculum for English.

Cracking Writing can be used to support most approaches to writing which recognise the benefit and importance of:

- reading and responding to model texts
- talk for writing and planning writing
- planning, drafting, editing and improving writing.

What's in it?

Cracking Writing offers nine writing units for each Year: four fiction units, four non-fiction units and one poetry unit. The units have been chosen to support the expectations of the National Curriculum for Key Stage 2 English. The units, and in particular the non-fiction units, can also be used as resources to enrich and complement your wider teaching. Each unit includes:

- a model text
- a reading comprehension activity in order to ensure close reading and comprehension of the model text
- active learning activities and guidance for six stages of teaching writing
- a framework for writing
- a detailed monitoring writing sheet which shows progression from 'below the expected standard' to 'working at greater depth' for the expected standard by the end of the academic year.

> Visit My Rising Stars online (www.risingstars-uk.com) to access your extra resources. These include:
> - model texts highlighted with key grammatical constructions
> - editable success criteria.

The text types and purposes of the units in *Cracking Writing* mirror those in Rising Stars' *Cracking Comprehension*. Each of the resources stands alone and is in no way dependent on the other, but schools that have both resources can add value to them by:

- seeing how well the children are able to apply strategies taught in *Cracking Comprehension* when faced with the new *Cracking Writing* text and additional comprehension questions
- using the *Cracking Comprehension* texts as additional model texts through which to explore the issues raised in *Cracking Writing* units.

How do I use it?

You can use the *Cracking Writing* units in any order. The pathway through each unit is flexible, according to the specific needs of you and your children. Whether you choose to follow through with one stage every day for six or seven days, or weekly for half a term or for a focused half day per half-term is your choice. The children will gain more from the sessions if they are closer together, but the decision rests with you – you know your class.

Each unit is divided into the same six stages. Depending on your own emphasis and the class's needs, you can allocate a lesson to each of the stages. You may wish to leave out some of the activities which don't address your priorities, but do check that the learning isn't needed for later in the unit.

However you choose to use the material, we recommend that you follow this process:

Stage 1: Introduce, read and respond to the model text

Each unit is based on a model text. These are generally extracts from good quality, age-appropriate children's fiction, non-fiction and poetry. Introductory activities start the children thinking about the subject matter of the text. Ideas generated are often used in a later stage.

Discussing children's responses to the model text and the comprehension questions will ensure the children are very familiar with the text for subsequent stages.

Stage 2: Analyse the text content (fiction)/analyse the text structure and organisation (non-fiction)

During this stage, children are asked to consider the setting, character and plot in the fiction model texts, and to explore the organisation, the order of ideas and the use of headings and other text features for the non-fiction texts. Children will work with response partners and groups for active learning activities aimed at co-constructing insights into the author's choices and their impact on the reader.

Stage 3: Analyse the text structure and language (fiction)/analyse the text purpose and language (non-fiction)

Activities in this stage are primarily focused on language, and the grammatical content and technical vocabulary for Year 6 in the National Curriculum, together with consolidation of grammatical content and vocabulary from previous years. The intention is to demonstrate how the grammar is used in texts and to consider the impact on the reader. Key grammatical constructions are highlighted on the model text (online at My Rising Stars). Paragraphs, cohesion and vocabulary are also considered in most units.

There are lots of opportunities for children to work in pairs or groups in order to encourage discussion and debate and to give all children the opportunity to share their ideas. You can decide whether you wish to work with a group of less confident children, or whether you wish to pair them with more confident peers.

Stage 4: Plan to write (including talk for writing)

The aim of this stage is to discuss ideas and create opportunities for drama, drawing, internet research, and so on, so that the children come to the writing session with a clear understanding of the content, style and vocabulary of what they want to write, whether the recommendation is a continuation of the model text or a piece of writing inspired by it.

- A framework for writing offers the children one way of recording key ideas they will find useful. A range of photocopiable frameworks are provided and some may be adaptable for use in other units.
- Each unit includes opportunities to 'talk like a writer'.
- Editable success criteria are available online at My Rising Stars. Agree and share the success criteria with the children.

Stage 5: Write (including talk for writing)

By the end of this stage, children will have completed their first draft, using their completed writing frameworks, results of 'talk like a writer' sessions and success criteria discussed in the previous stage. The activities give guidance on supporting the writing process, and children opportunities to read and make first corrections to their work.

- 🖥 This symbol is used to suggest where writing activities are particularly suited to being written on PCs/laptops/tablets.

Stage 6: Improve, edit, review and share the writing

For many children, it is the activities undertaken during this stage that have the greatest impact on their development as writers. They have recorded their ideas, so can now proofread, correct and improve their texts.

Photocopiable moderating writing sheets are provided on which you can highlight aspects of writing where children are working at the expected level and those which are below the expected level or working at greater depth. Each moderating writing sheet is slightly different to reflect the success criteria, and all reflect end-of-year expectations as the units can be completed in any order. During the first half of the year, most children will appear to be below expected levels.

My Family and Other Animals
Gerald Durrell

> In 1935, 10-year-old Gerald, his older brothers and sister and their mother moved to live on the Greek island of Corfu, together with their dog Roger. The book My Family and Other Animals is a partly autobiographical account of their adventures and was first published in 1956.

For some time, Mother had greatly envied us our swimming, both in the daytime and at night, but, as she pointed out when we suggested she join us, she was far too old for that sort of thing. Eventually, however, under constant pressure from us, Mother paid a visit into town and returned to the villa coyly bearing a mysterious parcel. Opening this she astonished us all by holding up an extraordinarily shapeless garment of black cloth, covered from top to bottom with hundreds of frills and pleats and tucks.

"Well, what d'you think of it?" Mother asked.

We stared at the garment and wondered what it was for.

"What is it?" asked Larry at length.

"It's a bathing costume, of course," said mother. "What on earth did you think it was?"

"It looks to me like a badly skinned whale," said Larry, peering at it closely.

"You can't *possibly* wear that, Mother," said Margo, horrified, "why, if looks as though it was made in nineteen-twenty."

"What are all those frills and things for?" asked Larry with interest.

"Decoration, of course," said Mother indignantly.

"What a jolly idea! Don't forget to shake the fish out of them when you come out of the water."

"Well, *I* like it, anyway," Mother said firmly, wrapping the monstrosity up again, "and I'm going to wear it."

"You'll have to be careful you don't get waterlogged, with all that cloth around you," said Leslie seriously.

"Mother, it's *awful*; you can't wear it," said Margo. "Why on earth didn't you get something more up to date?"

"When you get to my age, dear, you can't go around in a two-piece bathing-suit … you don't have the figure for it."

"I'd love to know what sort of figure that was designed for," remarked Larry.

"You really are *hopeless*, Mother," said Margo despairingly.

"But I *like* it … and I'm not asking you to wear it," Mother pointed out belligerently.

"That's right. You do what you want to do," agreed Larry; "don't be put off. It'll probably suit you very well if you can grow another three or four legs to go with it."

Mother snorted indignantly and swept upstairs to try on her costume. Presently she called to us to come and see the effect, and we all trooped up to the bedroom. Roger was the first to enter, and, on being greeted by this strange apparition clad in its voluminous black costume rippling with frills, he retreated hurriedly through the door, backwards, barking ferociously. It was some time before we could persuade him that it really was Mother, and even then he kept giving her vaguely uncertain looks from the corner of his eye. However, in spite of all opposition, Mother stuck to her tentlike bathing-suit, and in the end we gave up.

Unit 1: My Family and Other Animals

Name: Class: Date:

1. *"… and returned to the villa coyly bearing a mysterious parcel"*

   In this clause, tick **one** word that *coyly* is closest to in meaning.

   bravely ☐   quickly ☐

   proudly ☐   shyly ☐

2. What did Larry first suggest Mother's bathing costume looked like?

   _____

3. Draw lines to show each character's attitude to the bathing costume.

   Character   *Attitude*

   (Gerald (narrator))   (thinks it's old fashioned)

   (Larry)   (thinks it's a monstrosity)

   (Margo)   (scared of it)

   (Roger)   (amused but mystified by it)

4. Why is Mother indignant?

   _____

5. What was the *"strange apparition"* that Roger saw?

   _____

6. Explain how the descriptions given of the bathing costume justify both Mother's view towards it, and that of her children.

   Use evidence from the text to support your answer.

   _____

   _____

   _____

Unit 1 Using dialogue to clarify relationships and advance plot

In this unit children will:

- read a text where characters and their relationships are shown through dialogue
- identify everything they can learn about characters through description, dialogue and others' response to dialogue
- discuss the role of descriptive verbs and adverbs in enhancing the dialogue
- explore the impact of ellipses, semi-colons and parentheses as well as punctuation of dialogue
- plan, draft, edit and improve a description of another scene featuring the same characters.

Stage 1: Responding to the text

Activities:

- Establish prior knowledge. Show children a map so they can see the location of Corfu.
  - Have any of the children ever been on holiday to the Greek Islands, or know anyone who has?
  - Show pictures from the internet of Corfu. Discuss expectations about climate and life on the island.
- Remind children that this story is set just before the Second World War. If appropriate, find a couple of images of people on beaches, including ladies in swimsuits, from the 1920s and 1930s, to share with the children.
- Read the introduction to the text. Explain that Gerald Durrell grew up to be a famous naturalist, zookeeper and conservationist, and that a lot of the text in the book describes the wildlife he explored and learned about on Corfu. He has written several books. His brother, Larry (Lawrence Durrell), also became a very well-known writer for adults.
- Ensure the children understand the more ambitious/unusual language in the story, e.g. "coyly", "garment", "indignantly", "monstrosity", "belligerently", "apparition", "voluminous", "opposition" and "retreated". Consider whether any of these words would be useful in the children's writing and try to find ways to use them throughout the unit, encouraging the children to begin using them, too.
- Read and talk about the text.
  - Did the children find any bits of it funny? Which bits? Why?
  - Could this text have been written today? Is there any evidence that it was written over 60 years ago? Or that the events described happened over 80 years ago?
- Ask the children to answer the reading comprehension questions to ensure close reading of the text and good understanding.
- Together, share answers to the questions and discuss the strategies children used to answer them.

Resources needed:

Shared copy of the text (PDF/IWB/visualiser)

Images of Corfu

Each child needs:
- a copy of the text
- a copy of the comprehension questions.

Cracking Writing Year 6 · Unit 1

Stage 2: Analysing the text content

Activities:

- Ask children to read the text aloud to a response partner to revisit the text, develop fluency, ensure accurate pronunciation of all words and to practise reading with expression and a reasonable speaking pace.
- Ask children to underline any new words or phrases. Take feedback and explain what these mean in context.

Discussing characters

- Briefly, discuss the relationship between the children and their mother. Do they like her? Respect her? Laugh at her?
- Divide the class into four groups. (Each of these groups may wish to subdivide into pairs/threes and re-form to share outcomes.) Allocate:
  - a highlighter/pen/pencil colour to each group
  - one group to find out more about Larry and his relationship with Mother
  - one group to find out more about Margo and her relationship with Mother
  - one group (the slightly more difficult task) to find out more about Mother's relationships with her children
  - one group (the most difficult task) to find out more about the relationships between Gerry (the narrator) and his family.
- Ask each group to consider:
  - what their character says
  - what their character does
  - how their character responds to others and how others respond to them.
- Model finding information about Larry.
  - He says things like *"What is it?"* and *"It looks to me like a badly skinned whale"*.
  - He does things like: ask questions, say what he thinks, say funny things like *"It'll probably suit you very well if you can grow another three or four legs to go with it."*
  - How he responds to others: he doesn't speak to his brothers and sisters, only to Mother. He is interested in Mother's costume (*"What are all those frills and things for?" asked Larry with interest.*) and looks closely at it (*"Peering at it closely"*) but everything he says is making fun of it (e.g. *"Don't forget to shake the fish out of them when you come out of the water."*).
  - How others respond to him: his brothers and sister don't talk to him. Mother's response is to him and Margo. She starts by asking their opinions, then responds *"firmly"* (*"Well I like it, anyway," Mother said firmly*) then *"belligerently"* and ends up snorting *"indignantly"* and sweeping out of the room. But then she calls to her children to see the effect. This suggests that even if her feelings are hurt, she values his opinion.
    - Tell children to use their character's colour to underline all of the evidence in the text that shines a light on their character and who they are in the family.
    - Ask groups to use large sheets of paper to jot down their conclusions about their character.
- Once each group has found out everything they can, re-form the class into groups of approximately four, with one representative of each character group in each group of four. In their new groups children should:
  - share the insights gained in their character groups
  - use each character's colour to annotate the text to find the evidence to justify the conclusions reached.
- As a class, share the large sheets of paper with the conclusions about each character. Discuss whether there are any different or additional views or opinions about the characters. Remind children they need evidence to support their ideas.

Resources needed:

Shared copy of the text (PDF/IWB/visualiser)

Each group needs:
- flipchart/large paper and marker pens

Each child needs:
- a copy of the text
- highlighters/pens/pencils in four different colours (ideally, consistent colours for all children).

Discussing plot development

- Briefly, identify what has changed or developed in terms of the plot from the opening paragraph (after the introduction) to the end of the extract.
  - How much of the plot is told and how much shown through character's reactions?

Stage 3: Analysing the text structure

Activities:

Analysing dialogue

- Ask children to remind you about what an adverbial is (e.g. *a word or phrase that is used to modify a verb or clause*). Identify some adverbials from sentences from the text (e.g. "*Eventually, however, under constant pressure from us*, Mother paid a visit into town").
  - Together explore different ways in which the writer could have shared the same amount of information (e.g. *We put constant pressure on Mother. Eventually, she made a trip into town …*) Talk about the reasons why the writer might have chosen to include adverbials rather than have separate sentences.

Resources needed:

Shared copy of the text (PDF/IWB/visualiser)

Each child needs:
- the copy of the text they have previously highlighted and annotated
- a flipchart/large paper
- marker pens.

- Ask children to reread the text in groups of four. In each group, one child should read the words of the narrator, one of Larry, one of Margo and one of Mother. Let children take turns in reading the different roles.
  - Ask children how they knew the appropriate intonation to use each time they read. Ask them to circle all of the verbs and adverbials used to describe how the characters speak (e.g. "asked"; "asked … at length"; "said firmly").
  - Discuss the reasons why the narrator used adverbials as well as a range of verbs to describe how characters speak.
  - Discuss also the author's use of italics for emphasis. Was this helpful to children as they read? Why did the author include this information?
- Ask children to write a summary of the extract, omitting the dialogue.
  - Let them compare their summaries to the dialogue in the text.
  - Discuss why the author chose to use so much dialogue. What would be lost by recasting this as continuous text, rather than dialogue?

Analysing vocabulary

- Challenge pairs of children to find as many different ways as they can in the text of referring to the bathing costume. Include expanded noun phrases. Discuss why the author used so many different ways of referring to the costume. Make a note of the suggestions the children give and keep for use at Stage 4.

Analysing language

- Ask children to revisit the text, considering sentence length throughout. How does the fact that this is primarily dialogue influence sentence length and types of sentences?

Analysing punctuation

- Ask children to scan the text for less commonly used punctuation. Can they:
  - name the punctuation (e.g. *ellipses (…); semi-colon (;); parenthesis (in this text shown between commas)*
  - explain the purpose of each punctuation mark (*in this text semi-colons express a close relationship between the clauses on either side* ("Mother, it's awful; you can't wear it"); *ellipses indicate a pause* ("But I *like* it … and I'm not asking *you* to wear it") *and the information within the parenthetical commas is additional to the main clause – almost like an aside* (e.g. "Roger was the first to enter, and, on being greeted by this strange apparition clad in a voluminous black costume rippling with frills, he retreated")

Cracking Writing Year 6 · Unit 1

- suggest the alternatives that the author could have used (e.g. *in all instances, the author could have used full stops and separated the information*)
- discuss the impact of the choices the author made (e.g. *it gives the reader a clearer understanding of the relationship between the ideas that the author wanted to express*)?

• Direct children's attention to the inverted commas and to the range of punctuation used alongside. Ask pairs to identify and describe as many examples of different punctuation for dialogue as possible, e.g.
  - comma before closing, e.g. *"like a badly skinned whale," said Larry*
  - question mark before closing, e.g. *"… what do you think of it?" Mother asked*
  - full stop before closing, e.g. *"… and I'm going to wear it."*
  - lower case letter after opening, e.g. *"Well, I like it, anyway," Mother said firmly, … "and I'm going to wear it."*

Stage 4: Planning to write: Using dialogue to clarify relationships and advance plot

Activities:

- Introduce a scenario. *The same characters are sitting down to eat a meal. Mother has tried to experiment with cooking a meal of Greek dishes, but it has not been successful.* Explain to the children that they are going to be asked to write about the meal and the dialogue during it.
- Do any of the children know any Greek foods? (E.g. *moussaka, saganaki, stuffed vine leaves, kebabs, sheftalia (sausage), tzatziki, hummus, pita bread, Greek salads, feta cheese, baklava.*)
  - If possible, create the opportunity for children to taste some examples of Greek food and to describe the look, smell, taste and texture of the food.
  - Give pairs of children a short time to research Greek foods and to plan a simple meal they might like to try. (Or give a menu to the whole class of moussaka, hummus, pita bread, Greek salads with feta cheese, baklava and produce pictures of what it should look like.)
- Distribute the writing framework. Ask children to imagine different ways in which the menu they decided upon might go wrong.
  - Refer back to the list of phrases the children found for describing the bathing costume. Identify the simple noun phrases (e.g. *"the garment"*) and the noun phrases expanded with prepositional phrases (e.g. *"an extraordinarily shapeless garment of black cloth"*).
  - Together, model some expanded noun phrases to describe what the food might have looked like, based on some of the expanded noun phrases from the text (e.g. *"an extraordinarily shapeless garment of black cloth"* could help children structure their noun phrases, e.g. *an astonishingly shapeless pile of pink goop*).
- Suggest they jot down noun phrases expanded with prepositional phrases on their writing framework.
- Let children work in groups of four and allocate each one a character (Mother, Larry, Margo, Gerry).
  - Ask the children to improvise a meal-time conversation where they contribute as their characters. What kind of thing might each person complain about? How might they complain?
  - Ensure all children are given the opportunity to experiment with being more than one character.
  - Sample the children's ideas and note down any pieces of dialogue that really stand out to share with the class.

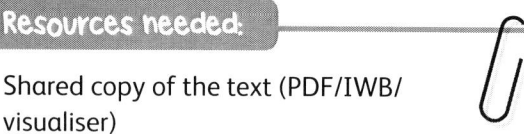

Resources needed:

Shared copy of the text (PDF/IWB/visualiser)

The success criteria

Each group needs:
- a flipchart showing character descriptions and information
- large paper
- the list of noun phrases from Stage 3

Each child needs:
- the copy of the text they have previously highlighted and annotated
- the writing framework from page 15 (some children may benefit from this being enlarged to A3).

- Give each group a large sheet of paper. Ask them to draw a cross to divide the paper into four equal spaces. They should label the spaces after each character.
- Model using the dialogue you noted when the children were participating in their improvisations, and recording it in the relevant spaces. Ask the children to help you work out what that character might have felt as they spoke.
- In the spaces, the group should record things they think each character might hear, say or feel.
- Give children time to move around the room to see whether anyone else has a word or an idea they could borrow.
- Split children into pairs (or threes). Within their planning pair, ask children to discuss and complete their writing frameworks, listing words, thoughts and feelings for each of the characters.
- Ask the children to consider and record how the dialogue progresses the plot of the episode (e.g. *they all eat up and pretend it's delicious; they feed it to Roger and go out to a restaurant; they all go and help Mother to cook another meal*).
- Ask the children to discuss what makes a successful dialogue and what they need to include in their story.
- Clarify the success criteria (online at My Rising Stars).

Stage 5: Writing

Activities:

- Remind children that the task is to write about a disastrous meal and the dialogue during it.
- Model writing an opening paragraph to set the scene – showing that the story is set in Corfu, and setting up the premise for the episode: Mother is cooking local dishes – but she has no idea how to cook them!
- Continue to model a paragraph involving some of the dialogue and expanded noun phrases you noted on your plan. Include interspersed description/action, adverbs that show how characters feel/speak and prepositional phrases.
- Give children a few minutes to 'talk like a writer' and tell their partner the opening and closing paragraphs of narrative as they plan to write it. If it helps, ask them to use a polite 'writer's voice'.
- Let response partners give some brief feedback before children swap roles.
- Read aloud the success criteria (online at My Rising Stars).
- Let the children write.
- Throughout the writing session, quietly let the children know how long they have spent, where in their story they should expect to be now and how long there is left.
- Five minutes before the end of the session, ask all children to stop writing and read their story aloud to themselves. If they find errors, missing words or words they can improve, they should use this opportunity to make changes.

Resources needed:

The success criteria

Each child needs:
- the copy of the text they have previously highlighted and annotated
- the completed writing framework.

Stage 6: Improving, editing, reviewing and sharing the writing

Activities:

- Revisit together the success criteria (online at My Rising Stars).
- Model the process below using your work as an example. The children can give you feedback on each step of the process. After you model a step, the children should have a go with their partner at editing their own work.

Resources needed:

Each child needs:
- the success criteria
- their writing/completed writing framework
- different coloured highlighters/pens.

Cracking Writing Year 6 · Unit 1

- Ask children to reread their texts three times with their response partner:
  - First read through: Children read their partner's text out loud to them. The child who wrote the text listens to check that their writing makes sense, listens out for obvious errors and checks that the text follows their plan. Children then swap roles.
  - Second read through: Children read their partner's text and highlight the success criteria they have met. They suggest three places where their partner could improve their work (to achieve or further improve on the success criteria).
  - Third read through: Children proofread their partner's text together with them. They check for errors in punctuation and spelling, and correct these as necessary. You should give input at this stage if needed.

Lessons from writing

- Prior to the session, identify errors that were commonly made. Write sample sentences that need to be corrected and ask the children to help you to fix them. These could include:
  - overuse of *said* or *asked* with no adverb to describe how the writer is feeling, e.g.
    - "What on earth is that?" asked Larry.
      "It's baklava of course," said Mother. "What did you think it was?"
      "I rather hoped it was for holding open doors," said Larry.
      "You don't expect us to eat it, do you?" asked Margo.

    Ask children first to suggest adverbs to add description to *said* and *asked* and then to suggest more powerful verbs.
  - two sentences used where one could combine the information more usefully using parenthesis, semi-colons or ellipsis, e.g.
    - Mother looked on proudly. We looked on in disbelief. Mother had cooked the meat in too hot an oven. She had bought the meat from a local butcher. "Well, I like it. And I'm not forcing you to eat it," Mother pointed out belligerently.

    Once children have explored the possible ways of punctuating the text, discuss what has been changed by the new punctuation and what would have been better left as it was.

Improving the writing

- **After the texts have been marked:** give the children time to read through your comments, to look at the success criteria and to implement any changes suggested. This should not involve the children rewriting the entire story – just those parts that you would like them to revisit to practise/improve their writing.

Share

Sometimes, children write stories to practise writing stories. Other times, there is a planned reason or an audience. If you want children to share their writing they can:

- rewrite it to presentation standards – however, this should be regarded simply as a handwriting activity, not as another opportunity to improve the text; the rewritten text should be used for a specific audience or display
- rewrite it on a computer – however this should be regarded as a keyboarding exercise
- publish their ideas in the form of a graphic novel
- recast their text as a playscript.

Unit 1: Using dialogue to clarify relationships and advance plot

| Name: | Class: | Date: |

Mother has tried to follow and adapt recipes to cook her family a Greek meal. The experiment has not been successful. What does each of the characters say and think?

Record expanded noun phrases that describe the dish/food and explain what has gone wrong.

What did **Larry** say?

What did he think?

What did **Margo** say?

What did she think?

What did **Gerry** (the narrator) say?

What did he think?

What did **Mother** say?

What did she think?

What will happen as a result of the conversation?

Unit 1: Moderating writing: Using dialogue to clarify relationships and advance plot

Name: Date:

		Contents	Text structure and organisation	Sentence structure	Vocabulary and descriptions	Punctuation	Spelling and handwriting
Working at greater depth within the expected standard		Characterisation of different characters is consistently recognised in the dialogue.	The level of formality in language used by different characters is maintained.	Grammatical structures are manipulated to maintain/change the level of formality.	Vocabulary is manipulated to maintain/change the level of formality.	A full range of taught punctuation is used, mostly accurately.	Handwriting is effortlessly fast, fluent and easy to read.
		Key characteristics of the main characters are expressed through their reaction to each other.	Paragraphs are used effectively to control pace.	At least one appropriate use of the passive voice to disguise/hide the agent is included.	Atmospheric setting is described using precise vocabulary, including figurative language.	Colons and/or semi-colons are used accurately.	Spelling – including of less familiar words – is generally accurate.
				A relative clause is used to add information.			
Working at the expected standard		Dialogue is interspersed with action and used to convey character and advance action.	Paragraphs are used effectively to sequence ideas.	Pronouns, adverbials and prepositional phrases are used appropriately to aid cohesion between sentences and paragraphs.	Vocabulary is generally appropriate to the level of formality within the text.	Some parenthesis is marked with commas, brackets or dashes.	Most words on the Year 5/6 list – or words of equivalent challenge – are correctly spelled.
				A wide range of clause structures is used, sometimes varying their position within the sentence.		Commas are used for clarity as well as in lists and after fronted adverbials.	Unstressed vowels are generally accurate.
				Parenthesis is used to add information.			
		Characters are consistently presented and well defined.	Clear plot development from the beginning to the end of the story is shown.	Conjunctions, adverbs and prepositions are used to link events.	Verbs, adverbs and adverbials describe how the character speaks or feels. Prepositional phrases add detail.	Largely correct use of inverted commas and associated punctuation is shown.	Legibility, fluency and speed determine which letters are left unjoined.
						Some use of colons or semi-colons is shown.	Handwriting is easily legible and may be sloped forwards for speed.
Working towards the expected standard		The story continues, based on the given characters and setting.	Paragraphs are generally used to organise ideas.	Pronouns and adverbials are used appropriately to aid cohesion between paragraphs.	The setting for the episode is clearly established.	Apostrophes are consistently used correctly.	Some words on the Year 5/6 list – or words of equivalent challenge – are correctly spelled.
		Dialogue is integrated and used (at least once) to convey character and advance action.	Events are told in a coherent sequence.	Conjunctions join clauses, adverbs/prepositions are used to show time passing.	Noun phrases are extended with adjectives and prepositional phrases.	Commas are used within a series of actions to clarify meaning.	In handwriting, most letters are appropriately joined.

Moon Bear

Gill Lewis

> Ma, Pa, Tam, Mae and Sulee live in Laos, near the border with Vietnam, which was heavily bombed during the Vietnamese War. The family has recently been forced to move from their home in the forested mountains to join a small village of peasant farmers.

Maybe it was because another full moon had passed since we were moved from our old village, but it began to really feel as if this could be our home here. The chickens had settled into their new roosts and we didn't need to corral the pigs to stop them wandering any more. Ma had traded flower-cloth on the highway for lamp oil and new nets to fish the Mekong. I'd killed six white-bellied rats for the pot with my slingshot. Ma was pleased, as we couldn't hunt bush-meat from the forest. Our old life in the mountains became like a distant memory. It didn't seem real any more, more like part of a dream.

Mae and Sulee had been for lessons with the new teacher who came to teach in the shade beneath the spreading branches of the flame tree. I didn't go with them. I had to help Pa in the fields, to clear the weeds and stones and dig the irrigation channels for the rice. We didn't have much time before the rains came.

I slung the pick and shovel across my back and headed out to the fields. My feet scuffed the hot earth. My mouth felt dry. Everything felt dry. I imagined the throat of the earth waiting for the rain. I imagined rain pitting the dust, filling up the cracks and ditches and streambeds. It wouldn't be long. The monsoon was coming. I could feel it. The dust in the air sparkled with it. One day soon, the rains would come.

I passed other villagers bent double, their wide-brimmed hats keeping off the sun. Our field was the furthest away, set back into the corner of a low hill. Pa had worked hard to clear the stones although we'd have to wait for the rains to soften the earth before we could plough and level it. He said we would plant fruit trees on the hill. Maybe even keep some bees. Not the wild ones, like in the forest, but we'd keep them in wooden hives. Pa understood bees. They understood him too.

I found him marking out the irrigation channel along the border of our field. In the monsoon, we would rely on water from the hills, but General Chan had promised us a water pump for the dry season. It meant we would be able to grow other crops all year too.

Pa straightened up, pushing his hands into the small of his back. "We need the handcart too, Tam. We have to move these stones."

I laid the pick and shovel on the ground next to him. "I'll get it now."

Pa wiped the sweat from his face. "And a drink, Tam. Bring water when you come back."

I ran along our field edge and only stopped when I reached the low rise of the hill. I turned back to look at Pa. He was stooped to reach the pickaxe. He looked out of place here. In our old village, my father was the Bee Man. He walked tall in the forests. He talked to the bees. The bees told him everything. But here, without the forest, my father was just a farmer, just a man.

Sunlight flashed on the pickaxe as he swung it high above his head.

Maybe if the forest bees had been here, they could have warned him. Maybe the bees would have seen the rusted metal casing hidden untouched beneath forty years of mud and weeds.

But there were no forest bees.

I watched the pick swing in a slow arc and sink into the ground.

There was no warning.

None.

The ground exploded and lifted up into the sky.

Mud and earth and stone rained down.

And when the dust cleared,
my father
the Bee Man,
was gone.

Unit 2: Moon Bear

Name:　　　　　　　　　　　　　　　　　　　Class:　　　　　Date:

1. List **three** pieces of evidence that the village was beginning to feel like home.

   _____

   _____

   _____

2. Circle the correct option to complete the sentence below.

   This story is told from the perspective of …

   Pa　　　　　Ma　　　　　Mae　　　　　Tam

3. Why do you think Pa pushed his hands into the small of his back as he straightened up?

   _____

4. Write evidence for each statement to show how life has changed since the family moved.

Before when they lived in the forest	Now they live near a hill
The family ate bush-meat.	
Pa was the Bee Man.	

5. Do you think the family is having an easy life?

   Use at least **three** pieces of evidence from the text in your answer.

   _____

   _____

   _____

6. Why do you think the author chose to use such short lines at the end of the text?

   _____

   _____

   _____

Cracking Writing Year 6 · Unit 2

Unit 2 Developing a story within its setting

In this unit children will:
- read an extract from a story where the setting is key
- identify information about the setting and appreciate its importance to the story
- create a timeline, unpicking flashbacks in the narrative
- look for different ways in which the author achieves cohesion within and between paragraphs
- identify the impact of different types of sentences, including passives
- place, draft, edit and improve a story in which setting is key.

Stage 1: Responding to the text

Activities:

- Establish prior knowledge. Show children a map so they can see the location of Laos.
  - What do children know about the Vietnamese War? (E.g. 1960s America vs Vietnam; cluster bombs dropped by America, some of which exploded and did great damage.)
  - What do children know/predict about crops from Southern Asia? Do they know how rice is grown? (E.g. *In paddy fields when they are swamped by rains.*)
  - Do they think the people who grow the rice are likely to be rich or poor? Discuss their answers.
  - What do they know about the monsoon? (E.g. *Annual period of very heavy rainfall in a country that is otherwise hot and dry.*)
- Explain that this is an extract from early on in a much longer story.
- Ensure the children understand the more ambitious/unusual language in the story, e.g. "roosts", "corral", "irrigation", "monsoon". Tell the children the meaning of any new vocabulary and encourage them to use the word in a sentence to establish the meaning in context, e.g. *The farmer dug an irrigation ditch to carry water around the field.*
- Read and talk about the text.
  - Establish an understanding of the idea of 'peasant farmers' (*subsistence: eat what you grow with a bit extra for trading*) and their lifestyles.
  - What do children think happened to Pa at the end? Explain that this scene in the novel is setting up the reason behind Tam having to leave his family and go to work in a particularly cruel place.
- Ask the children to answer the reading comprehension questions to ensure close reading of the text and good understanding.
- Together, share answers to the questions and discuss the strategies children used to answer them.

Resources needed:

Shared copy of the text (PDF/IWB/visualiser)

Each child needs:
- a copy of the text
- a copy of the comprehension questions.

Cracking Writing Year 6 · Unit 2

Stage 2: Analysing the text content

Activities:

- Ask children to read the text aloud to a response partner to revisit the text, develop fluency, ensure accurate pronunciation of all words and to practise reading with expression and a reasonable speaking pace.
- Ask children to underline any new words or phrases. Take feedback and explain what these mean in context.

Resources needed:

Shared copy of the text (PDF/IWB/visualiser)

Each group needs:
- a flipchart/large paper

Each child needs:
- a copy of the text
- coloured highlighters/pencils.

Discussing setting

- Begin to model making notes about the family's life in their new home. With the children's help, identify information which you should include in your notes and that which can be left out. Remind children that notes do not have to be in sentences and can use symbols, such as arrows, and layout as well as words.
- Ask children to work in pairs to write brief notes summarising what they now know about the life of a peasant rice-farmer in Laos.
- Use information from the first paragraph to model highlighting information about the setting.
- Pairs should then revisit the text to highlight key information relating to the setting of the story. Remind them that setting includes aspects like time and weather as well as things and places.
- Discuss the importance of the setting to the story: could this story have happened here, where you live? Why?
- Let groups of children agree on the *key* details the author has given us to make the setting come alive and which helps us to visualise and imagine it. Talk about the language used (e.g. *"in the shade beneath the spreading branches of the flame tree"*; *"The dust in the air sparkled with it"*) and identify examples of figurative language (e.g. *"the throat of the earth waiting for the rain"*).
- Identify which information is told and which is shown, e.g. how do we know that: it's very hot, very dry, the ground is stony?

Discussing plot development

- Using large sheets of paper, ask groups of children to create a timeline of Tam's life and experiences, using only what they know, or can deduce, from the text extract. Challenge them to think about what it was like living in the mountains, what it is like in the new village, his hopes for the future and the potential implications of Pa's death.
- From the first paragraph, model highlighting information relating to Tam's emotions, his pride in his memories, his current reality and his hopes for the future. Include ideas which are explicit (e.g. *"Ma was pleased"*) as well as those which can be inferred (e.g. *"our old life … became more like a distant memory"*). Ask children in their pairs to continue highlighting this kind of information.
- Talk about why the author weaves Tam's emotions, pride in his memories about his father's skills, current reality and hopes for the future throughout the extract of a longer text.
- Link that to a consideration of why the author chose to tell this story as a first person narrative. What gains does it bring? What information does it potentially limit?

Stage 3: Analysing the text structure

Activities:

Analysing paragraphs and cohesion

- Together, compose a brief summary of the information in the first paragraph. Remind children that summaries should be clear and concise, should be written in sentences and should only include the most important information and ideas.
- Ask groups of children to draw two wide columns on their paper.
  - In column 1, ask them to summarise what happens in each paragraph. (For this purpose, treat all the text from *"There was no warning"* to the end as one paragraph.)
  - In column 2, ask them to look for cohesive devices which link these events to events in previous paragraphs (e.g. *use of pronouns and possessive determiners such as "his", "their", "my", reference to information, time adverbials or prepositions*). Remind them that the links may be to earlier paragraphs than the immediately preceding one.
  - Are there any paragraphs with no clear links to any other paragraphs?
- Look in more detail at the end of this extract from *"There was no warning"*. Discuss the impact of spreading the final sentence over four lines.

Analysing vocabulary

- Challenge pairs of children to find vocabulary that explicitly places the story within its setting (e.g. *"fish the Mekong"; "hunt bush-meat"; "flame-tree"*). Discuss the impact of this very specific vocabulary.

Analysing language

- Ask children to identify the brief dialogue (paragraphs 6–8) and consolidate rules for punctuation and layout.
- Discuss how the dialogue is integrated and advances the action of the story. Ask children to identify the key things we learn from this brief dialogue and clarify that, importantly, it gives a reason why Tam would not be at the scene when the bomb explodes.
- Ask children to revisit the text, considering sentence length throughout. How does the fact that this is told in the first person influence sentence length?
- Check that children know how to identify the passive voice, e.g.
  - Can you add the phrase 'by someone' somewhere after the verb and the sentence still makes sense, e.g. *we were moved from our old village by someone*?
  - Is there part of the verb *to be* together with a past participle (*e.g. were moved*), the subject of the sentence is not doing the verb (in *"we were moved from our old village"*, 'we' are not doing anything)?
- Challenge children to spot passive constructions in the text (in the introduction: *"the family had ... been forced"* and *"was heavily bombed"*). Discuss why the author has used these constructions at specific points. Ask children to consider whether it matters to the story who performed these actions.

Resources needed:

Shared copy of the text (PDF/IWB/visualiser)

Each group needs:
- a flipchart/large paper

Each child needs:
- the copy of the text they have previously highlighted
- marker pens.

Stage 4: Planning to write: Developing a story within its setting

Activities:

- Discuss the fact that this story is closely linked to its setting of a rice farm in Vietnam; it couldn't happen in this way in a village in the UK. Tell children that they are going to select a setting, then think about a story that could only take place in it (e.g. only in an African river or lake could someone by threatened by hippos).
- Together, consider a story set by an African lake. Ask children to suggest words and phrases that might describe the setting, then suggest outline plots in that setting. Model making notes.

Cracking Writing Year 6 · Unit 2

- Give each group of children a large sheet of paper. Ask them to draw a cross to divide it into four equal spaces. They should label three spaces with three geographical settings (select settings children are likely to be familiar with, either through first-hand experience or films, e.g. desert, jungle, sea, island, mountains, etc.).
- Ask each group to use one colour of pen to create a word bank of useful and specific words and phrases for each of their settings in the spaces. Using a different colour of pen, they should record plot ideas.
- Give children a few minutes to move around and see whether anyone else has a word or an idea they could borrow. They can then return and annotate their group's paper accordingly.
- Ask the children to think of a setting they would like to write about and find a partner (or form a group of three) with someone who would like to develop a plot in the same setting.
- Model outlining the main points of one of the African lake plot ideas children suggested earlier. Take ideas from the children, reminding them that each action affects possibilities later in the story (e.g. *if someone's leg is eaten by a crocodile, they can't then climb a tree*).
- Within their planning pair/group, ask children to discuss possible plots and to agree on a broad plot outline. Remind them that the plot should be relevant to the setting. The children should talk through the entire plot, making joint decisions on what happens.
- Distribute the writing framework and ask each child to complete the first three boxes.
- Ask them to revisit the paragraph summaries they wrote at Stage 3. They should then write out a paragraph-by-paragraph summary of their story.
- Ask the children to discuss what makes a successful story which is specific to a setting and what they need to include in their story.
- Clarify the success criteria (online at My Rising Stars).

Resources needed:

Shared copy of the text (PDF/IWB/visualiser)
The success criteria
Groups of children need:
- a flipchart/large paper and different coloured pens/pencils

Each child needs:
- the copy of the text they have previously highlighted
- the paper on which they noted paragraph summaries at Stage 2
- the writing framework from page 25 (some children may benefit from this being enlarged to A3).

Stage 5: Writing

Activities:

- Remind children that the task is to write a story that could only take place in its setting.
- Use the plan you made at Stage 4 and model writing an opening paragraph to establish the setting and introduce the characters. As you write, explain how you are creating cohesion within and between paragraphs, include noun phrases expanded by prepositional phrases as well as adverbs to add detail and precision and find at least one opportunity to use the passive voice. Explain to the children why you used it.
- Give children a few minutes to 'talk like a writer' and use their plan to tell their partner the story as they plan to write it. If it helps, ask them to use a polite 'writer's voice'.
- Let response partners give some brief feedback before children swap roles.
- Read aloud the success criteria (online at My Rising Stars).
- Let the children write.
- Throughout the writing session, quietly let the children know how long they have spent, where in their story they should expect to be now and how long there is left.

Resources needed:

The success criteria
Each child needs:
- the copy of the text they have previously highlighted
- the completed writing framework.

Cracking Writing Year 6 · Unit 2

- Five minutes before the end of the session, ask all children to stop writing and read their story aloud to themselves. If they find errors, missing words or words they can improve, they should use this opportunity to make changes.

Stage 6: Improving, editing, reviewing and sharing the writing

Activities:

- Revisit together the success criteria (online at My Rising Stars).
- Model the process below using your work as an example. The children can give you feedback on each step of the process. After you model a step, the children have a go with their partner at editing their own work.

Resources needed:

The success criteria

Each child needs:
- their writing/completed writing framework
- different coloured highlighters/pens.

- Ask children to reread their texts three times with their response partner:
  - First read through: Children read their partner's text out loud to them. The child who wrote the text listens to check that their writing makes sense, listens out for obvious errors and checks the text follows their plan. Children then swap roles.
  - Second read through: Children read their partner's text and highlight the success criteria they have met. They suggest three places where their partner could improve their work (to achieve or further improve on the success criteria).
  - Third read through: Children proofread their partner's text together with them. They check for errors in punctuation and spelling, and correct these as necessary. You should give input at this stage if needed.

Lessons from writing

- Prior to the session, identify errors that were commonly made. Write sample sentences that need to be corrected and ask the children to help you to fix them. These could include:
  - overuse of noun phrases when pronouns or possessive determiners would clarify relationships and add cohesion, e.g.
    - *The hippos opened their mouths wide. The hippos' mouths were much bigger than I had thought. The hippos' mouths were fuller of teeth than I could have imagined. The hippos were also fast swimmers. As I struggled through the water, I could see that the hippos were gaining on me.*
  - missed opportunities to use the passive voice, e.g. *I knew that a determined enemy was following me; the storm had easily overwhelmed the little boat; the choppy waves were slowly drowning me.*
    - Ask children to recast these sentences using the passive and consider how the meaning and emphasis changes.
    - Can they hide the agent in some of the sentences (e.g. *I knew that I was being followed; the little boat had been easily overwhelmed; I was slowly being drowned*)? What is the impact of doing so?

Improving the writing

- **After the texts have been marked**: give the children time to read through your comments, to look at the success criteria and to implement any changes suggested. This should not involve the children rewriting the entire story – just those parts that you would like them to revisit to practise/improve their writing.

Share

Sometimes, children write stories to practise writing stories. Other times, there is a planned reason or an audience. If you want children to share their writing:
- they can publish their different stories in a themed collection for the class library
- they can work together to create a themed background upon which to display their texts
- pairs with similar stories could try making a simple animation, reading their story aloud as the narrative.

Unit 2: Developing a story within its setting

Name:　　　　　　　　　　　　　　　　　Class:　　　　　Date:

Setting: —————————————————————

Useful words, phrases and details:

Brief plot outline:

Main characters and their key characteristics (e.g. *age, gender, state of mind*, etc.):

Summarise each of your paragraphs:

Unit 2: Moderating writing: Developing a story within its setting

Name: Date:

	Contents	Text structure and organisation	Sentence structure	Vocabulary and descriptions	Punctuation	Spelling and handwriting
Working at greater depth within the expected standard	A sense of tension/threat/suspense is developed.	Events at the end of the text are linked to previous actions.	Grammatical structures are manipulated to maintain/change the level of formality.	Vocabulary is manipulated to maintain/change the level of formality.	A full range of taught punctuation is used, mostly accurately.	Handwriting is effortlessly fast, fluent and easy to read.
	Key characteristics of the main characters are expressed through dialogue, description and reasons.	Paragraphs are used effectively to control pace.	At least one appropriate use of the passive voice to disguise/hide the agent and create a sense of powerlessness is included.	Atmospheric setting is described using precise vocabulary including expanded noun phrases and figurative language.	Colons and/or semi-colons are used accurately.	Spelling – including of less familiar words – is generally accurate.
Working at the expected standard	Dialogue is integrated and used (at least once) to convey character and advance action.	Paragraphs are used effectively to organise ideas.	Pronouns, adverbials and prepositional phrases are used appropriately to aid cohesion between sentences and paragraphs.	Vocabulary is generally appropriate to the level of formality within the text.	Some parenthesis is marked with commas, brackets or dashes.	Most words on the Year 5/6 list – or words of equivalent challenge – are correctly spelled.
			A wide range of clause structures is used, sometimes varying their position within the sentence.		Commas are used for clarity as well as in lists and after fronted adverbials.	Unstressed vowels are generally accurate.
	The story is well placed in its setting.	Events are linked and clear plot development from the beginning to the end of the story is shown.	The passive voice is used (at least once) to hide the agent of the action.	Adverbs, prepositional phrases and expanded noun phrases add detail and precision.	Largely correct use of inverted commas and associated punctuation is shown.	Legibility, fluency and speed determine which letters are left unjoined.
			Some parenthesis is marked with commas, brackets or dashes.		Some use of colons or semi-colons is shown.	Handwriting is easily legible and may be sloped forwards for speed.
Working towards the expected standard	The setting of the model text is described.	Paragraphs are generally used to organise ideas.	Pronouns and adverbials are used appropriately to aid cohesion between paragraphs.	The setting for the story is clearly established.	Apostrophes are consistently used correctly.	Some words on the Year 5/6 list – or words of equivalent challenge – are correctly spelled.
		Events are told in a coherent sequence.	Fronted adverbials at the beginning of paragraphs indicate a change of time or place.	Noun phrases are extended with adjectives and prepositional phrases.	Commas are used within a series of actions to clarify meaning.	In handwriting, most letters are appropriately joined.

Into the Future

Adapted from *The Time Machine* by H. G. Wells

> In this extract, based on *The Time Machine* by H. G. Wells, a character called the Time Traveller tells the story of his voyage into the future, in a time machine he has built himself.

It was at ten o'clock today that the first of all Time Machines began its career. I gave it a last tap, tried all the screws again, put one more drop of oil on the quartz rod, and sat myself in the saddle. I drew a breath, set my teeth, gripped the starting lever with both hands, and went off with a thud.

Soon, the laboratory got hazy and went dark. I pressed the lever over to its extreme position. The night came like the turning out of a lamp, and in another moment came tomorrow. I am afraid I cannot convey the peculiar sensations of time travelling. They are excessively unpleasant. There is a feeling exactly like one has upon a switchback – of a helpless headlong motion! I felt the same horrible anticipation, too, of an imminent smash.

As I put on pace, night followed day like the flapping of a black wing. The slowest snail that ever crawled dashed by too fast for me. As I went on, still gaining velocity, the palpitation of night and day merged into one continuous greyness; the sky took on a wonderful deepness of blue; the jerking sun became a streak of fire, a brilliant arch, in space.

The landscape was misty and vague. I saw trees growing and changing like puffs of vapour, now brown, now green; they grew, spread, shivered, and passed away. I saw huge buildings rise up faint and fair, and pass like dreams. The whole surface of the earth seemed changed, melting and flowing under my eyes.

At first I hardly thought of stopping, hardly thought of anything but these new sensations. But presently a fresh series of impressions grew up in my mind – a certain curiosity and with it a certain dread. And so my mind came round to the business of stopping.

I lugged over the lever. The time machine went reeling over, and I was flung headlong through the air. There was the sound of a clap of thunder in my ears. I may have been stunned for a moment.

Presently I remarked that the confusion in my ears was gone. A pitiless hail was hissing around me. I was on what seemed to be a little lawn, surrounded by rhododendron bushes. As the columns of hail grew thinner, I saw a colossal carved figure. It was of white marble, in shape something like a winged sphinx, but the wings, instead of being carried vertically at the sides, were spread so that it seemed to hover. The face was towards me; the sightless eyes seemed to watch me; there was the faint shadow of a smile on the lips.

As I looked up at the crouching white shape, the full audacity of my voyage came suddenly upon me. What might appear when that hazy curtain of hail was withdrawn? What might have happened to men? What if the race had developed into something inhuman, unsympathetic, and overwhelmingly powerful?

Already I saw other vast shapes – huge buildings with intricate parapets and tall columns. I was seized with fear. I felt naked in a strange world. I set my teeth and grappled fiercely with the machine. It gave under my desperate efforts and turned over.

But with this recovery of the machine my courage returned. I looked more curiously and less fearfully at this world of the remote future. In a circular opening, high up in the wall of the nearer house, I saw a group of figures clad in rich, soft robes. They had seen me, and their faces were directed towards me.

Then I heard voices approaching me. Coming through the bushes by the White Sphinx were the heads and shoulders of men running.

Unit 3: Into the Future

Name:					Class:			Date:

1. *"As I put on pace, night followed day like the flapping of a black wing."*
   What do you think the author is trying to say in using this image?

   _____

2. Tick **three** things we know to be true of the carved figure described in the extract.

   It was made of marble. ☐

   Part of it was like a horse. ☐

   Its wings were spread out. ☐

   It was like a sphinx. ☐

   It was beautiful. ☐

3. Why do you think the Time Traveller's courage returned when he had recovered the time machine?

   _____

4. How would you describe the Time Traveller's feelings after his journey through time? Tick **one**.

   He is not surprised by what he finds. ☐

   He is worried about what he will find. ☐

   He is enjoying his adventure. ☐

   He does not know how he will get the time machine working again. ☐

5. *"At first I hardly thought of stopping, hardly thought of anything but these new sensations."*
   In this sentence, tick **one** word that *sensations* is closest to in meaning.

   bumps ☐			locations ☐
   experiences ☐		dreams ☐

6. **Find** and **copy two** pieces of evidence that show the Time Traveller is worried about what he will find in the place where he has arrived.

   _____

   _____

Cracking Writing Year 6 · Unit 3

Unit 3: Writing a science fiction/fantasy story

In this unit children will:
- read part of a science fiction story
- consider the differences between fantasy and science fiction, and the impact on the ability of the reader to predict outcomes
- identify key features of the setting and how they could impact on the plot development
- consider the impact of the author's use of vocabulary in descriptions
- explore how sentence style and length are involved in moving the plot forward
- plan, draft, edit and improve a fantasy or science fiction story.

Stage 1: Responding to the text

Activities:

- Establish prior knowledge of science fiction and fantasy texts and films.
    - How are science fiction and fantasy similar and dissimilar?
    - Have children read books and played computer games which are grounded in science fiction or fantasy? Ask them to share their experiences.

Resources needed:

Shared copy of the text (PDF/IWB/visualiser)

Each child needs:
- a copy of the text
- a copy of the comprehension questions.

- Introduce the text title. Draw a class mind map of children's predictions about the book, based on the title and the idea that it is either science fiction or fantasy.
- Isaac Asimov, a famous sci-fi writer, said that: *science fiction, given its grounding in science, is possible; fantasy, which has no grounding in reality, is not.*
    - *Think, pair, share:* According to this definition, is this story fantasy or sci-fi? Ask children for evidence to support their ideas.
- Before reading, ensure the children understand the more ambitious/unusual language in the story, giving them examples of the words/phrases in context, e.g. *"laboratory"*, *"convey"*, *"excessively"*, *"the palpitation of night and day"*, *"audacity"*, *"the remote future"*. Talk about what images these words and phrases bring to mind.
- Read and talk about the text.
    - Could this text have been written today? Is the idea of travelling through time in a machine like this still plausible? Is there any evidence that it was written over 100 years ago?
- Ask the children to answer the reading comprehension questions to ensure close reading of the text and good understanding.
- Together, share answers to the questions and discuss the strategies children used to answer them.

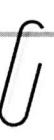

Stage 2: Analysing the text content

Activities:

- Ask children to read the text aloud to a response partner to revisit the text, develop fluency, ensure accurate pronunciation of all words and to practise reading with expression and a reasonable speaking pace.
- Ask children to underline any new words or phrases. Take feedback and explain what these mean in context.

Discussing setting

- Divide the board into two columns. Head one 'Familiar' and the other 'Unfamiliar'. Model finding one or two details from the text which are familiar to us or the author (e.g. *"a little lawn"*) and unfamiliar (e.g. *the carved figure and the description of the humans in the future*). Ask the children to help you to identify the evidence in the text to support your assertions. Talk about the images the words create in the children's minds (remembering that some children will be more drawn to images and some more drawn to words).
- Organise the class into small groups. Give each a large sheet of paper and pens. Ask them to divide the paper into two columns.
  - On one side, they should record any details of the setting that are familiar.
  - On the other, ask for details that are unfamiliar.
  - At the same time, they should underline the evidence on their copies of the story, using different colours for familiar and unfamiliar features.
- Compare the groups' answers and clarify discrepancies.
- Discuss why the author includes both the familiar and the unfamiliar when creating a setting (e.g. *there is sufficient that is familiar for children to be able to visualise the future setting, but sufficient that is unfamiliar for children to recognise that they can't predict what will happen in the fantasy setting*).

Discussing plot development

- Talk about a standard plot shape for a story:
  - introduction (*characters, setting, back story*)
  - problem (*what will drive the story forwards*)
  - action (*addresses the issue identified in the problem*)
  - outcome (*how the action finishes*)
  - ending (*ties up loose ends and refers back to problem*).
- Within this plot structure, the extract of the story is from the transition between identifying the problem (travelling through time) and the action (the Time Traveller's experiences in the future).
- Ask groups to suggest what might follow this extract, building on what we know from the text about the setting and characters.
- Give opportunities to share ideas. Encourage the rest of the class to give feedback on others' ideas, considering how the ideas incorporate what is already known. Make a note of the ideas so they can be referred to later.

Resources needed:

Shared copy of the text (PDF/IWB/visualiser)

Each group needs:
- a flipchart/large paper and marker pens

Each child needs:
- a copy of the text
- pens/pencils in two different colours (ideally, consistent colours for all children).

Cracking Writing Year 6 · Unit 3

Stage 3: Analysing the text structure

Activities:

Analysing vocabulary

- Discuss what the children see in their minds when they read the description of the narrator's journey through time. What techniques does the author use? Consider:
    - Is the use of similes and other techniques effective?
    - Is he trying to help the reader to understand more clearly?
    - Is he trying to extend the reader's vocabulary?
    - Are there other reasons?
    - What is the impact of the description of time travel on the reader?

Resources needed:

Shared copy of the text (PDF/IWB/visualiser)

Each child needs:
- the copy of the text they have previously annotated
- highlighters/pens/pencils in four different colours.

Analysing paragraphs and cohesion

- Ask children what they understand by the term 'cohesion' when discussing texts, e.g. *A text has cohesion if it is clear how the meanings of its parts fit together.* Cohesive devices that can help to do this include:
    - *determiners and pronouns – which refer back to previous words*
    - *conjunctions and adverbs – which make relationships between ideas clear*
    - *referral to things previously mentioned.*
- Work with children to identify examples of each cohesive device as a class before they work in their groups.
- Ask different groups of children to look for cohesive devices. Allocate one group to look at each of these aspects:
    - the distribution of pronouns in and between paragraphs
    - the use of determiners such as *a/an* to introduce new features or object and *the/these* to notify the reader that the features have been met previously
    - references to things/people/events that were mentioned in previous paragraphs
    - adverbials, conjunctions and prepositions as transitional words, either fronted or within sentences
    - repetition of a key term or the use of a synonym for it.
- Ask the group who identified pronouns to demonstrate on the shared text how pronouns referred back and forth to different noun phrases. Select a noun phrase (e.g. "the time machine") and together track all the references to it through the text.
- Ask children from the different groups to make new groups to share what they have found out. All children should annotate their texts, using different colours to track ideas through the text.
- Discuss how these – and any other cohesive devices children identified – help the reader to follow ideas through and between the paragraphs.

Analysing language

- Ask children to revisit the text, considering sentence length throughout.
    - How does sentence length vary? Look at the sentence length for descriptions and compare with sentences that describe actions.
    - Why does sentence length vary? Consider when the sentences are reflecting the Time Traveller's thoughts and where they are about his observations, feelings or actions. Compare the sentence length when the author is describing the setting or characters with descriptions of the action.

Cracking Writing Year 6 · Unit 3

Stage 4: Planning to write: Writing a science fiction/fantasy story

Activities:

- Before the session, decide whether you want children to write a complete story, or to continue this one.
- Explain that you want the children to continue/write a science fiction/fantasy story set in a place that is both familiar/Earth-like and unfamiliar/not Earth-like.
- Distribute the writing framework. If you want to continue this story, ask the children to use known information to complete all boxes up to the box headed 'Action' on the writing framework.
- If you want children to begin new stories, ask them to work in pairs/small groups according to the types of story they want to write, e.g.
  - stories entirely set in space/a science fiction world
  - stories entirely set in a fantasy world
  - stories set on Earth but with fantasy characters or elements
  - stories set on Earth but with science fiction elements.
- If you wish to place restrictions on their work, such as text length, limits to violence, etc., impose these now before children develop their ideas. Clarify your expectations about the type of story you want children to write.
- Begin by modelling a sketch of the setting for a story you would write. Draw and/or label elements which are familiar/Earth-like or unfamiliar/not Earth-like. Discuss how you could use these fantasy elements in your plot.
- Within their pairs/groups ask children to draw and label, or to list, fantastical/science fiction elements in a setting they would like to use.
- In another colour, ask them to annotate their work to show how the fantastical/science fiction elements contribute to plot development.
- Make time for the children to look at each other's ideas and ask questions so that children have to clarify their ideas.
- Model completing the writing framework for the ideas you sketched and discussed earlier.
- Ask children to use the ideas from their drawings, together with clarifications from discussions with peers, as they record their ideas.
- Give children time to tell their story, working through their plan, to a response partner. Ask the response partner to:
  - identify whether the story makes sense, with clear links between ideas
  - check that the telling will be reasonable in the length of text to be written
  - suggest any vocabulary or improvements that could easily be implemented.
- Ask the children to discuss what makes a successful science fiction/fantasy story and what they need to include in their story.
- Clarify the success criteria (online at My Rising Stars).

Resources needed:

Shared copy of the text (PDF/IWB/visualiser)

The success criteria

Each group needs:
- large paper

Each child needs:
- the copy of the text they have previously highlighted
- the writing framework from page 36 (some children may benefit from this being enlarged to A3)
- different coloured pens/pencils.

Cracking Writing Year 6 · Unit 3

Stage 5: Writing ✏️

Activities:

- Remind children that the task is to continue/write a science fiction/fantasy story.
- Model writing an opening paragraph to set the scene – showing the setting and introducing the plot as you planned it. Continue to model a paragraph including dialogue integrated to advance the action, devices that will aid cohesion (pronouns, adverbials, prepositional phrases), the passive voice and descriptive verb choices.
- Give children a few minutes to 'talk like a writer' and tell their partner the opening and closing paragraphs of narrative as they plan to write it. If it helps, ask them to use a polite 'writer's voice'.
- Let response partners give some brief feedback before children swap roles.
- Read aloud the success criteria (online at My Rising Stars).
- Let the children write.
- Throughout the writing session, quietly let the children know how long they have spent, where in their story they should expect to be now and how long there is left.
- Five minutes before the end of the session, ask all children to stop writing and read their story aloud to themselves. If they find errors, missing words or words they can improve, they should use this opportunity to make changes.

Resources needed:

The success criteria

Each child needs:
- the copy of the text they have previously highlighted and annotated
- the completed writing framework.

Stage 6: Improving, editing, reviewing and sharing the writing ✏️

Activities:

- Revisit together the success criteria (online at My Rising Stars).
- Model the process below using your work as an example. The children can give you feedback on each step of the process. After you model a step, the children should have a go with their partner at editing their own work.
- Ask children to reread their texts three times with their response partner:
  - First read through: Children read their partner's text out loud to them. The child who wrote the text listens to check that their writing makes sense, listens out for obvious errors and checks the text follows their plan. Children then swap roles.
  - Second read through: Children read their partner's text and highlight the success criteria they have met. They suggest three places where their partner could improve their work (to achieve or further improve on the success criteria).
  - Third read through: Children proofread their partner's text together with them. They check for errors in punctuation and spelling, and correct these as necessary. You should give input at this stage if needed.

Resources needed:

Each child needs:
- the success criteria
- their writing/completed writing framework
- different coloured highlighters/pens.

Lessons from writing

- Prior to the session, identify errors that were commonly made. Write sample sentences that need to be corrected and ask the children to help you to fix them. These could include:
  - dialogue providing an additional commentary on the action, e.g.
    - "Let's go and see what's in the cave," suggested Oscar. They went into the cave and saw a shape. "Look at that shape," said Gail." "I wonder what it is." They went to look more closely at the shape.

- Challenge children to decide how they want the action to proceed and then to use the dialogue to create it, rather than stating both action and dialogue.
  - pronoun references are unclear, e.g.
    - *"I can't believe this," said Ahmed. Mikael stared at his feet because he couldn't bear to watch. He took a step backwards and tripped over him.*
    - It's easy to write passages like this when you can 'see' the action inside your head, but it needs to be clear to the reader too. Can the children help to clarify what might be going on?

Improving the writing

- **After the texts have been marked**: give the children time to read through your comments, to look at the success criteria and to implement any changes suggested. This should not involve the children rewriting the entire story – just those parts that you would like them to revisit to practise/improve their writing.

Share

Sometimes, children write stories to practise writing stories. Other times, there is a planned reason or an audience. If you want children to share their writing they could:

- make an audio-recording, possibly with an appropriate soundtrack
- develop it into a drama for others to watch
- repackage it as a brief for a screenplay
- rewrite it to presentation standard; however, this should be regarded simply as a handwriting activity not as another opportunity to improve the text – the rewritten text should be used for a specific audience or display.

Unit 3: Writing a science fiction/fantasy story

Name: Class: Date:

Think about how the setting and characters in your story are both familiar and unfamiliar. Make notes in the table below.

	Familiar/Earth-like	Unfamiliar/not Earth-like
Setting How will your setting be Earth-like/not Earth-like?		
Character Which characters will be Earth-like/not Earth-like and how?		

Make notes for each part of your fantasy or science fiction story.

Introduction (characters, setting, back story)	
Problem (What will drive the story forwards?)	
Action (addresses the issue identified in the problem)	
Outcome (how the action finishes)	
Ending (ties up loose ends and refers back to problem)	

Unit 3: Moderating writing: Writing a science fiction/fantasy story

Name: Date:

	Contents	Text structure and organisation	Sentence structure	Vocabulary and descriptions	Punctuation	Spelling and handwriting
Working at greater depth within the expected standard	There is a good balance between description and action throughout the story.	Paragraphs are used effectively to control pace.	Sentences of different lengths are used effectively for different purposes throughout.	Atmospheric setting is described using precise vocabulary including expanded noun phrases and figurative language.	A full range of taught punctuation is used, mostly accurately.	Handwriting is effortlessly fast, fluent and easy to read.
	The fantasy/science-fiction elements of the story are well integrated and clearly linked.	A wide range of cohesive devices effectively link ideas between and within paragraphs.	At least one appropriate use of the passive voice with the intention of disguising/hiding the agent to create an effect is included.	Careful choice of details limits unnecessarily lengthy descriptions	Colons and/or semi-colons are used accurately.	Spelling – including of less familiar words – is generally accurate.
Working at the expected standard	Dialogue is integrated and used (at least once) to advance action.	Paragraphs are used effectively to organise ideas.	Pronouns, adverbials and prepositional phrases are used appropriately to aid cohesion between sentences and paragraphs.	Some more sophisticated vocabulary is used to support the reader in 'seeing' the setting.	Some parenthesis is marked with commas, brackets or dashes.	Most words on the Year 5/6 list – or words of equivalent challenge – are correctly spelled.
						Unstressed vowels are generally accurate.
	The story is well placed in its setting, with links between fantasy/science-fiction elements and plot development.	Cohesive devices link ideas between and within paragraphs.	At least one sentence is written using the passive voice.	Adverbs, prepositional phrases and expanded noun phrases add detail and precision.	Commas are used for clarity as well as in lists and after fronted adverbials.	Legibility, fluency and speed determine which letters are left unjoined.
			Parenthesis is used to add information.		Largely correct use of inverted commas and associated punctuation is shown.	
					Some use of colons or semi-colons is shown.	Handwriting is easily legible and may be sloped forwards for speed.
Working towards the expected standard	The story includes some fantasy/science-fiction elements in the action.	Paragraphs are generally used to organise ideas.	Pronouns and adverbials are used appropriately to aid cohesion between paragraphs.	The setting for the story is clearly established.	Apostrophes are consistently used correctly.	Some words on the Year 5/6 list – or words of equivalent challenge – are correctly spelled.
	Some dialogue is used in the story.	Events are told in a coherent sequence.	Fronted adverbials at the beginning of paragraphs indicate change of time or place.	Noun phrases are extended with adjectives and prepositional phrases.	Commas are used within a series of actions to clarify meaning.	In handwriting, most letters are appropriately joined.

Cracking Writing Year 6 © Rising Stars UK Ltd 2017. You may photocopy this page.

Macbeth

Retold by Marcia Williams

> *Macbeth, a Scottish general, had just led his army to victory in the name of Macbeth's cousin, King Duncan. On his way back to report to the king with his friend Banquo, Macbeth met three witches who prophesied that he would become King of Scotland.*

In the days that followed, Macbeth could think of nothing but the crown – the crown of Scotland that would sit on his head when he was the king! How soon would that be, he wondered. Should he be doing something to make sure it happened? No, he thought to himself. "If chance will have me king, why, chance may crown me, without my stir." But the seed of ambition had been sown by the three witches, and ambition is an evil master. Dark thoughts began to stir in Macbeth's mind – thoughts of ways he could hasten the day of his coronation.

When Banquo and Macbeth finally arrived at the palace, King Duncan could not have greeted them more warmly or with more gratitude for their great bravery. "O worthiest cousin! Welcome hither!" he cried. "I have begun to plant thee, and will labour to make thee full of growing. Noble Banquo, that hast no less deserved, let me infold thee and hold thee to my heart."

Such a greeting from the king would have swelled the hearts of most men, but not Macbeth's. For shortly afterwards, King Duncan named his son, Malcolm, heir to the throne of Scotland. This was the honour that Macbeth had been hoping to receive.

"Stars, hide your fires!" Macbeth muttered to himself, "Let not light see my black and deep desires."

King Duncan went on to say that he would visit Macbeth's castle at Inverness. Again, Macbeth should have been pleased by this honour. But now he was consumed by the desire to be king and all he could think about was that Malcolm now stood in his way. Maybe he could not rely on chance to make him king … maybe he would have to give chance a helping hand!

Macbeth couldn't wait to tell his wife all that had happened, so he sent a letter ahead to her. Her excitement grew as she read it, for she was even greedier for power than Macbeth. She could already see the golden crown of Scotland on her husband's head. Macbeth was ambitious, but he had a sense of honour. Lady Macbeth was quite ruthless and only honoured power and ambition. She was capable of destroying anyone who stood in her husband's way.

By the time Macbeth reached the castle, Lady Macbeth was already plotting King Duncan's death! When she greeted Macbeth she saw that his thoughts had also turned to murder, but she was worried by his lack of cunning. "Your face, my thane, is a book where men may read strange matters," she warned him. "Look like the innocent flower, but be the serpent under't."

Their talk was interrupted by the arrival of King Duncan and his two sons, Prince Malcolm and Prince Donalbain. The king was delighted by the sweet air around the castle, and by Lady Macbeth, who appeared so charming and welcoming. But Lady Macbeth was secretly urging her husband to kill him that night.

In preparation for the evil deed, Lady Macbeth drugged King Duncan's two guards, who lay beside the king as he slept.

Now that murder had become a reality, Macbeth was agonising over it. King Duncan was a good and gentle man, and a guest in Macbeth's house. It was his duty to protect the king, not murder him.

"We will proceed no further in this business," he told his wife. "If we should fail?"

"Screw your courage to the sticking-place and we'll not fail!" Lady Macbeth scorned.

So, swayed by his wife, Macbeth reluctantly agreed to murder the king as he lay in bed that night. Lady Macbeth's evil heart swelled with satisfaction and she retired to her chamber to await the time.

...

Reluctantly, Macbeth picked up the daggers. Closing his eyes, he plunged them into King Duncan's heart. Then he ran from the room, his hands dark with the king's blood and the daggers still clenched in his fists.

"I have done the deed," he cried, overwhelmed with the horror of it.

Unit 4: Macbeth

Name:　　　　　　　　　　　　　　Class:　　　　　　　　　　Date:

1. List **two** things King Duncan did which showed that he honoured Macbeth.

   _____

   _____

2. *"If chance will have me king, why, chance will crown me without my stir."*

   In this sentence, tick **one** word that *chance* is closest to in meaning.

   fate ☐   danger ☐

   change ☐   time ☐

3. What did Macbeth plan that would give *"chance a helping hand"*?

   _____

4. Find and copy **one** similarity and **one** difference between Macbeth and his wife.

   _____

   _____

5. What did Lady Macbeth do to show she could *"Look like the innocent flower, but be the serpent under't."*?

   _____

   _____

6. Do you think the author blames Lady Macbeth or Macbeth more for the murder of King Duncan?

   Use evidence from the text to support your answer.

   _____

   _____

Unit 4 — Retelling part of a story

In this unit children will:

- read a retelling of part of Macbeth
- sketch important plot moments, identifying when key decisions were made that influenced subsequent actions
- find out about characters from their actions and the actions of those around them
- consider how the author integrated Shakespeare's language and vocabulary
- identify cohesive devices and evaluate their impact; look at sentence structure (including passives and modal verbs) and evaluate their impact
- plan, draft, edit and improve the same actions, but told from the viewpoint of a different character.

Stage 1: Responding to the text

Activities:

- Establish prior knowledge of Shakespeare.
- Introduce the title of Shakespeare's *Macbeth*. Draw a class mind map of children's knowledge or understanding of the story. If necessary, offer a very brief summary of the plot.
- Read the introduction to the text. Have the children heard any of the witches' rhymes before, e.g.

  "When shall we three meet again? In thunder, lightning or in rain?"

  "Double, double toil and trouble; Fire burn and cauldron bubble."

- If appropriate, read some of the witches' lines to the children.
- Clarify the difference between telling/creating a story and retelling.
- Explain that in this retelling of the play, all of the words said by the characters were written by Shakespeare, but Marcia Williams has retold the story, mostly in her own words.
- Check that the children understand the archaic language before reading: *"hasten"* (hurry up), *"thee"* (you), *"hither"* (here) as well as the meaning of less common words such as: *"agonising"* (painful), *"cunning"* (clever) and *"infold"* (hug).
- Read and talk about the text. Discuss, in particular, the dialogue, demystifying Shakespeare's words as necessary.
- Ask the children to answer the reading comprehension questions to ensure close reading of the text and good understanding.
- Together, share answers to the questions and discuss the strategies children used to answer them.

Resources needed:

Shared copy of the text (PDF/IWB/visualiser)

Each child needs:

- a copy of the text
- a copy of the comprehension questions.

Plot summary

Witches predict Macbeth will become King of Scotland.

He and his wife murder King Duncan.

Duncan's sons flee for their lives.

Macbeth is crowned king.

Anyone, including his friends, who Macbeth thinks may suspect him is slain. This includes the wife and children of his friend Macduff.

Macbeth and Lady Macbeth are both driven mad by guilt. Lady Macbeth dies.

Macduff leads his army against Macbeth and kills him.

Duncan's older son, Malcolm, is crowned King of Scotland.

Cracking Writing Year 6 · Unit 4

Stage 2: Analysing the text content

Activities:

- Ask children to read the text aloud to a response partner to revisit the text, develop fluency, ensure accurate pronunciation of all words and to practise reading with expression and a reasonable speaking pace.
- Ask children to underline any new words or phrases. Take feedback and explain what these mean in context.

Resources needed:

Shared copy of the text (PDF/IWB/visualiser)

Each group needs:
- a flipchart/large paper and marker pens

Each child needs:
- a copy of the text
- highlighters/pens/pencils in three different colours (ideally, consistent colours for all children).

Discussing plot

- *Think, pair, share:* Do children think this retelling is focused more on developing setting, character or plot? Ask them to provide evidence to back up their statements.
- Remind children of work they have done previously on summarising stories. Tell children you want them to sketch out the key plot points as a way of creating picture summaries of the action. Discuss what would go in the first 'frame'. Use stick figures and labels to demonstrate that the task is sketching, not detailed drawing.
- In small groups, tell children to create a series of sketches of the key plot points from the battle mentioned in the introduction to the end of this extract.
  - Let groups compare what they did with others.
    - Did they draw the same number of frames?
    - Did they identify the same plot points?
  - Discuss the choices the children made, focusing as much on what was excluded from their picture summaries as much as what they decided to include.
- Together, identify key moments in the plot when Macbeth could have made a different decision but was guided by others.

Discussing character

- Focus on the character of Macbeth. Model finding information about him from what he says, what he does and what others say or think about him. Identify information we are told (e.g. *Macbeth thought of nothing but the crown*) and information that we are shown through his actions and other people's reactions (e.g. *that he's easily influenced by what he hears*).
- Divide children into character groups: Macbeth, Lady Macbeth, King Duncan. Allocate a highlighter/pen/pencil colour to each character group. Within each group, children should:
  - annotate their text, underlining all the evidence they can find about their character
  - draw up a list of attributes on a large sheet of paper, and beside each attribute tell us whether we are shown it (mark with S) or told it (mark with T).
- Invite one 'expert witness' from each character group to explain to the class what they found out about their character.
- Discuss the author's view of each of the characters.
  - How do we know what the author thinks?
  - How are we as readers influenced by the author's viewpoint?

Discussing setting

- What do we know about the setting for this retelling of the story?
- Model finding information about Macbeth's home. Start to highlight evidence in the text (e.g. *"castle at Inverness"; "the sweet air around the castle"*).
  - Ask children in pairs to continue to find and highlight evidence about the setting.

- Does it matter in terms of the events in the plot that we know comparatively little about the setting? Invite children to consider:
    - that this was originally a playscript; why might there be less description in a play?
    - in a retelling of a play, what the narrator is most likely to focus on: setting, plot or character, and discuss why.

Stage 3: Analysing the text structure

Activities:

Analysing vocabulary

- Choose one of the Shakespearean words/quotation and talk about how it works within the original play and within this retelling.
- Discuss why the author decided to integrate Shakespeare's own words throughout. Remind children that *Macbeth* is a playscript (which is mostly dialogue) and that this is a retelling of the story told in the play.
    - What is the impact of the decision to use Shakespeare's words?
    - Do children think it is successful? Ask them to explain their answers.
- Revisit the dialogue, translating one of the quotations into modern English. Then ask pairs of children to translate each part of the dialogue into more modern language.
    - How much can they understand of it? What are the clues they are using to work it out?
    - How would the text be different if those words were not in Shakespeare's language at all?

Resources needed:

Shared copy of the text (PDF/IWB/visualiser)

Each child needs:
- the copy of the text they have previously highlighted and annotated
- coloured highlighters/pens/pencils.

Analysing paragraphs

- Discuss paragraph length. Most paragraphs are fairly short. What is the impact on the pace of the plot development of this succession of shorter paragraphs?
- Discuss the opening sentences of each paragraph. Remind children that in non-fiction, topic sentences summarise the development of an idea in the paragraph. This is less often found in fiction. Do children think these opening sentences are acting as brief summaries of the action? Discuss the impact of this.

Analysing cohesion

- Ask children what they understand by the term 'cohesion' when discussing texts, e.g. *A text has cohesion if it is clear how the meanings of its parts fit together. Cohesive devices that can help to do this include:*
    - *determiners and pronouns – which refer back to previous words*
    - *conjunctions and adverbs – which make relationships between ideas clear*
    - *referral to things previously mentioned.*
- Work with children to identify examples of each cohesive device as a class before they work in their pairs or groups.
    - Model finding an example each of:
        - pronouns or determiners
        - adverbials, conjunctions and prepositions as transitional words
        - repetition of a key term or the use of a synonym for it
        - references to things/people/events that were mentioned in previous paragraphs.
    - Are there any parts of the text where it is *not* clear who or what is being referred to? (E.g. *Consider the final paragraph. What does "plunged them into King Duncan's heart" – refer to? His eyes? The sleeping guards? The daggers?*)
    - How would they alter the text to clarify?

Cracking Writing Year 6 · Unit 4

- Ask pairs of children to look for cohesive devices.
  - Ask children to annotate their texts, using colour to show how ideas progress through the text.
- Discuss how these – and any other cohesive devices children identified – help the reader to follow ideas through and between the paragraphs.

Analysing language

- Ask children to identify the longest sentence in the extract (*paragraph 2, the sentence beginning "When Banquo and Macbeth finally arrived …" is 27 words long*). Which other long sentences did the children find? Talk about when in the plot these longer sentences are used, and when there are mostly shorter sentences. Discuss the impact on the reader.
- Can children remember the signs of a passive construction? (*You can find or insert the words 'by someone' somewhere after the verb; you will see part of the verb 'to be' together with a past participle; the subject of the sentence is not the person doing the action.*) Identify one of the passive constructions in the text (e.g. "*is crowned*" in the chapter title).
  - Challenge children to spot passive constructions in the text. Discuss why the author used these constructions at these points. Ask children to consider whether it matters to the story who performed these actions.
- Can children tell you examples of modal verbs which are used to express probability or possibility? (E.g. *will, would, can, could, may, might, shall, should, must, ought.*) Identify "*could*", "*would*" and "*should*" in the first paragraph.
  - Ask children to scan the text for further examples of modal verbs.
  - Discuss where they are in the text and why they are used (e.g. *mostly when Macbeth is dithering about whether to kill the king or not; once Macbeth has reached home, and is being guided by his wife, the tone becomes more certain*).

Analysing punctuation

- Check that children are familiar with punctuation – dashes, semi-colons, ellipses and apostrophes – and can tell you what they indicate. Ask children to scan the text and highlight examples. (Note Shakespeare's poetic use of apostrophes for more contractions than are used today in English, e.g. "*under't*"). Take feedback and discuss how this punctuation is used.
- Draw children's attention to places where commas are used before closing inverted commas and where other punctuation is used. Discuss any confusion or questions about speech punctuation.

Stage 4: Planning to write: Retelling part of a story

Activities:

- Before the session, decide whether you want children to recast this episode from a specific point of view or to retell a different story from an unusual point of view (e.g. *Three Billy Goats Gruff*). If you choose that they retell a different story, create a new version of the writing framework and populate the main events column.
- Ask children to revisit the character studies presented by the groups at Stage 2. Ask each group's expert witness to recap their group's findings.
- Tell the children their task, e.g. to retell the events described in the text but from a different viewpoint. Discuss how this could change the story.
- *Think, pair, share:* What will change if we retell an event from a different viewpoint (e.g. *actions and characters involved won't change, but an understanding of motivation and thoughts will*).

Resources needed:

Shared copy of the text (PDF/IWB/visualiser)

The success criteria

Each child needs:

- to see character studies created at Stage 2
- the copy of the text they have previously highlighted and annotated
- their graphic retellings from Stage 2 of the writing process
- the writing framework from page 47 (some children may benefit from this being enlarged to A3).

- Model reimagining the meeting between Duncan and Macbeth from Duncan's point of view. How does he feel about Macbeth? What does he think Macbeth will feel on hearing news about Malcolm? Or on hearing that the king is going to honour him with a visit to his castle? Make notes to record your ideas.
- Distribute the writing framework. Explain that you want pairs of children to decide what each of the characters (or their supporters) would think of each of the events listed.
- Ask children to revisit their graphic retelling from Stage 2. Which other events do they think should be listed? Ask them to create boxes for additional events on the reverse of the sheet, numbering all the boxes to show their order.
- Discuss the completed boxes. Identify how the different characters responded to the events.
- Model transferring your imagining of Duncan honouring Macbeth into the relevant box on the writing framework.
- Within their pairs/groups, ask children to go through each of the events they identified and think about how it was viewed by the characters. Remind them they only need to make notes.
- Model using your notes to retell the events in the story from Duncan's point of view.
- In their pairs, ask each child to choose a character and then to tell the events from their character's view – it can be a first person account (e.g. a diary entry) or a third person retelling which is sympathetic to one of the characters, but not the other two. Remind children that they will need to:
  - build up/justify their own position
  - relate all relevant plot points.
- Give children time to tell their story, working through their plan, to a response partner. Ask the response partner to:
  - identify whether the story makes sense, and has clear links between ideas
  - check that the telling will be reasonable in the length of text to be written
  - suggest any vocabulary or improvements that could easily be implemented.
- Ask the children to discuss what makes a successful retelling from a particular character's point of view and what they need to include in their story.
- Clarify the success criteria (online at My Rising Stars).

Stage 5: Writing

Activities:

- Remind children that their task is to rewrite the events from the model text but from the point of view of a different character.
- Model writing an opening paragraph from the notes you made in the previous session, retelling the events from the point of view of Duncan. Include: dialogue integrated to advance the action; a passive form which muddies the water as to who carried out an action; modals to express possibility; devices that will aid cohesion (pronouns, adverbials, prepositional phrases); and descriptive verb choices.
- Give children a few minutes to 'talk like a writer' and tell their partner the opening and closing paragraphs of narrative as they plan to write it. If it helps, ask them to use a polite 'writer's voice'.
- Let response partners give some brief feedback before children swap roles.
- Read aloud the success criteria (online at My Rising Stars).
- Let the children write.
- Throughout the writing session, quietly let the children know how long they have spent, where in their story they should expect to be now and how long there is left.
- Five minutes before the end of the session, ask all children to stop writing and read their story aloud to themselves. If they find errors, or missing words or words they can improve, they should use this opportunity to make changes.

Resources needed:

The success criteria

Each child needs:
- the copy of the text they have previously highlighted and annotated
- the completed writing framework.

Cracking Writing Year 6 · Unit 4

Stage 6: Improving, editing, reviewing and sharing the writing

Activities:

- Revisit together the success criteria (online at My Rising Stars).
- Model the process below using your work as an example. The children can give you feedback on each step of the process. After you model a step, the children should have a go with their partner at editing their own work.

Resources needed:

Each child needs:
- the success criteria
- the writing/completed writing framework
- different coloured highlighters/pens.

- Ask children to reread their texts three times with their response partner:
   - First read through: Children read their partner's text out loud to them. The child who wrote the text listens to check that their writing makes sense, listens out for obvious errors and checks the text follows their plan. Children then swap roles.
   - Second read through: Children read their partner's text and highlight the success criteria they have met. They suggest three places where their partner could improve their work (to achieve or further improve on the success criteria).
   - Third read through: Children proofread their partner's text together with them. They check for errors in punctuation and spelling and correct these as necessary. You should give input at this stage if needed.

Lessons from writing

- Prior to the session, identify errors that were commonly made. Write sample sentences that need to be corrected and ask the children to help you to fix them. These could include:
   - inconsistent point of view of character, e.g.
      - King Duncan saw Macbeth and hugged him, thinking what a brave man he was. Macbeth was thinking how quickly he could kill Duncan. Duncan said proudly "I know that you will be pleased that Malcolm will be my heir." Macbeth smiled on the outside but scowled on the inside because he wanted to be the heir.
      - Discuss how the text can be recast to reflect just one character's thoughts.
   - modal verbs not used to express possibility, so the text reads as more certain than it should, e.g.
      - "My husband will be King of Scotland," thought Lady Macbeth. "He will kill Duncan, then he will be king and I will be queen. Is he strong enough to kill Duncan? I will help him to do it."
      - Together, explore how language of possibility and dreaming can be used to create stronger text.

Improving the writing

- **After the texts have been marked:** give the children time to read through your comments, to look at the success criteria and to implement any changes suggested. This should not involve the children rewriting the entire story – just those parts that you would like them to revisit to practise/improve their writing.

Share

Sometimes, children write stories to practise writing stories. Other times, there is a planned reason or an audience. If you want children to share their writing they could:
- rewrite it as a playscript
- draw their character and display their story next to the drawing
- use their story as a resource for a mock trial of Lady Macbeth and Macbeth.
- rewrite it to presentation standard; however, this should be regarded simply as a handwriting activity not as another opportunity to improve the text – the rewritten text should be used for a specific audience or display.

Unit 4: Retelling part of a story

Name: Class: Date:

Make notes about what each character thought, did or felt at each point in the plot. Add more plot points on the back of this sheet if you think they are important. The first one is done for you.

Plot point	Characters
Witches prophecy Macbeth will be King of Scotland.	Macbeth: Should I do something about this? Lady Macbeth: I should do something about this! Duncan (or his supporters): know nothing about it.
Macbeth and Banquo arrive at the royal palace and are honoured by King Duncan.	Macbeth: Lady Macbeth: Duncan (or his supporters):
Macbeth arrives back at his own castle and talks to his wife.	Macbeth: Lady Macbeth: Duncan (or his supporters):
King Duncan arrives at Macbeth's castle.	Macbeth: Lady Macbeth: Duncan (or his supporters):
Macbeth and his wife carry out the murder.	Macbeth: Lady Macbeth: Duncan (or his supporters):

Cracking Writing Year 6 © Rising Stars UK Ltd 2017. You may photocopy this page.

Unit 4: Moderating writing: Retelling part of a story

Name: Date:

	Contents	Text structure and organisation	Sentence structure	Vocabulary and descriptions	Punctuation	Spelling and handwriting
Working at greater depth within the expected standard	There is a good balance between character and action throughout the retelling.	Paragraphs are used effectively to control pace.	Sentences of different lengths are used effectively for different purposes throughout.	Precise vocabulary including expanded noun phrases and figurative language is included.	A full range of taught punctuation is used, mostly accurately.	Handwriting is effortlessly fast, fluent and easy to read.
	The characterisation and justifications of the viewpoint character are consistent maintained.	A wide range of cohesive devices effectively link ideas between and within paragraphs.	At least one appropriate use of the passive voice to disguise/hide the agent is included.	Careful choice of details limits unnecessarily lengthy descriptions.	Colons and/or semi-colons are used accurately.	Spelling – including of less familiar words – is generally accurate.
Working at the expected standard	Clear plot development involves all main events identified.	Paragraphs are used effectively to organise ideas.	Pronouns, adverbials and prepositional phrases are used appropriately to aid cohesion between sentences and paragraphs.	Vocabulary is generally appropriate to the level of formality within the text.	Some parenthesis is marked with commas, brackets or dashes.	Most words on the Year 5/6 list – or words of equivalent challenge – are correctly spelled.
	Dialogue is used to create character and progress the plot.				Commas are used for clarity as well as in lists and after fronted adverbials	Unstressed vowels are generally accurate.
	The characterisation of the main character is well expressed.	Cohesive devices link ideas between and within paragraphs.	Modal verbs are used to express possibility.	Adverbs, prepositional phrases and expanded noun phrases add detail and precision.	Largely correct use of inverted commas and associated punctuation is shown.	Legibility, fluency and speed determine which letters are left unjoined.
			At least one sentence is written using the passive voice.		Some use of colons or semi-colons is included.	Handwriting is easily legible and may be sloped forwards for speed.
Working towards the expected standard	The story includes most identified elements of the plot.	Paragraphs are generally used to organise ideas.	Pronouns and adverbials are used appropriately to aid cohesion between paragraphs.	Some accurate vocabulary is used to create characterisation.	Apostrophes are consistently used correctly.	Some words on the Year 5/6 list – or words of equivalent challenge – are correctly spelled.
	There is evidence to identify the viewpoint character.	Events are told in a coherent sequence.	Fronted adverbials at the beginning of paragraphs indicate change of time or place.	Noun phrases are extended with adjectives and prepositional phrases.	Commas are used within a series of actions to clarify meaning.	In handwriting, most letters are appropriately joined.

Ancient and Medieval Art

Rosie Dickens

Many beautiful works of art survive from Ancient times – from Egyptian tomb paintings to Minoan palace decorations. But the earliest artists would not have thought of their work as 'art' the way we do today. Most early art was actually made for ritual or magic purposes.

Walk like an Egyptian

Egypt was ruled by kings, called pharaohs, from about 3000 BCE to 30 BCE. Much of the art that survives from that period was made for tombs, including carved stone statues and elaborately detailed paintings.

The ancient Egyptians believed that art had magical powers. They decorated tombs with images of everyday life, because they really believed these would help the person live on in the next world. People thought it was more important to record details clearly than to create natural-looking scenes. For them, art was a way of preserving life. In fact, one Egyptian word for sculptor can be translated as "he-who-keeps-alive".

A depiction of a painting in an Egyptian tomb.

Island art

From about 2000 BCE, art flourished on the Greek islands, particularly on Crete, where a people called the Minoans lived. The Minoans were great seafarers and traded with the Egyptians, and their art shows an Egyptian influence. But the Minoan style was less stiff and formal.

A lot of Minoan art was to do with religious rituals. For example, many statues show gods or worshippers. But some Minoan art – such as animal designs on storage jars – was probably just for decoration. So, for the first time, people were making art for its own sake, just because they liked the way it looked.

Artists and warriors

Then, from about 1600–1100 BCE, a people known as Mycenaeans dominated most of Greece. They were great warriors and fought many battles, including the Trojan War. You can see their preoccupation with war reflected in their art, which often shows warriors and fight scenes.

The Mycenaeans took over Crete from the Minoans, and were influenced by their art too. But compared with Minoan art, Mycenaean paintings seem much less fluid. The difference between the two styles shows how early Greek art developed and changed, unlike Egyptian art, which remained virtually the same for thousands of years.

The art of observation

The ancient Greeks were fascinated by the world around them and studied it closely – and they used their observations of real life in their art. Sculptors of the period tried to show the human body in a realistic, natural-looking way. The standards they set, for both beauty and technical skill, have been admired and imitated for centuries.

Unfortunately, very few Greek paintings have survived. Paintings made on wood rotted away, and wall paintings were lost when buildings were destroyed. But we know quite a lot about Greek painting from ancient writings. And the Greeks were famous for making painted vases and dishes, many of which did survive.

A Greek sculpture of an athlete preparing to throw a discus.

Unit 5: Ancient and Medieval Art

Name: Class: Date:

1. Why was the earliest art we know about not thought of as "art"?

   _____

2. How did the Minoans know about art in Egypt?

   _____

3. "… unlike Egyptian art which remained virtually the same for thousands of years"

   In this clause, tick **one** word that *virtually* is closest to in meaning.

   | beautifully | ☐ | nearly | ☐ |
   | exactly | ☐ | scarcely | ☐ |

4. How did the Ancient Greeks change art?

   _____

5. Put one or more ticks in each row to show which statements are true for the Ancient Egyptians, Minoans, Mycenaeans and Greeks.

	Egyptians	Minoans	Mycenaeans	Greeks
Art was used for ritual purposes.				
Artists painted pictures of animals.				
The style was influenced by Ancient Egyptian art.				
Artwork tried to show what people and animals really looked like.				
Images were painted on walls or storage jars.				

6. Why do you think the writer chose to organise the information in the order shown in the text?

   _____

Cracking Writing Year 6 © Rising Stars UK Ltd 2017. You may photocopy this page.

Unit 5 Writing a formal information text

In this unit children will:
- read a formal information text, comparing information from different parts of the text, and identify the organising principles
- consider paragraphs, topic sentences and their function
- find features of formal language, including passives, and consider their impact
- identify a wide range of punctuation for a range of sentence types
- plan, draft, edit and improve a formal information text.

Stage 1: Responding to the text

Activities:

- In pairs, ask children to come up with a definition of 'art'. As they work, ask them to consider questions like:
  - What is the function of art? (*For the artists to express their emotions, or for the audience to feel emotion? Simply for enjoyment of artists/audience?*)
  - Which media do they associate with art? (E.g. *paint, crayons, clay, wood, film, photography, architecture, science, music, gymnastics, cooking/baking …*)
  - Does everyone have to like the work of art?
  - Does the artist have to intend to create 'art', or could a dog with a paintbrush attached to its tail be called an artist?
  - Does there have to be skill for someone to produce 'art'?

  Clarify that there are no 'right' answers to the questions, but they should help the children to think about art.

- Ask children what the oldest piece of 'art' is they have seen images of. Was that art a sculpture, in a picture frame, on a storage jar, etc?
- Before you read the text together, explain that BCE means 'before common era', i.e. before we started numbering the years from year 0. (This is sometimes referred to as BC – Before Christ – but BCE is more inclusive of different religions, cultures and beliefs.)
- Before you read the text, ensure the children understand the more ambitious/unusual language, e.g. "architecture", "influenced", "elaborately", "flourished", "observation", "dominated", "preoccupation", "reflected in their art", "paintings seem much less fluid" and "imitated". Tell the children the meaning of any new vocabulary and ask them to use it in contextual sentences.
- Read the text together and discuss:
  - whether the children think that the author has the same view of art as the one they have
  - how art changed between the Ancient Egyptians and the Ancient Greeks.
- Ask the children to answer the reading comprehension questions to ensure close reading of the text and good understanding.
- Together, share answers to the questions and discuss the strategies children used to answer them.

Resources needed:

Shared copy of the text (PDF/IWB/visualiser)

Each child needs:
- a copy of the text
- a copy of the comprehension questions.

Stage 2: Analysing the text structure and organisation

Activities:

- Ask children to read the text aloud to a response partner to revisit the text, develop fluency, ensure appropriate pronunciation of all words and to practise reading with good intonation and expression.
- Ask children to underline any new words or phrases. Take feedback and explain what these mean in context.

Resources needed:

Shared copy of the text (PDF/IWB/visualiser)

Each child needs:
- a copy of the text
- coloured highlighters/pen/pencils.

Analysing text structure

- Ask children to discuss the headings. Why did the author not give the following headings to these sections: 'Ancient Egyptians', 'Minoans', 'Mycenaeans' and 'Ancient Greeks'? (*What makes the reader most likely to read on? The names of historical periods they may never have heard of, or a short description of the people?*)
- Can children tell you why the author organised the sections in this way? (*It's more or less chronological. Look at the dates together and remind children that, like negative numbers, the number of years BCE get smaller as they become more recent, so 2000 BCE is much older than 200 BCE.*)

Identifying progression of ideas

- Select two of the sections of the text and model ways of comparing and contrasting the information in them. In particular, demonstrate how to make notes about the ideas that link the sections (see below).
- Organise the children into four groups, and challenge each group to compare and contrast the ideas in two sections:
  - *Walk like an Egyptian* and *Island art*
  - *Island art* and *Artists and warriors*
  - *Artists and warriors* and *The art of observation*
  - *Walk like an Egyptian* and *The art of observation* (this is the most challenging comparison).
- Ask children to make annotations/notes about the ideas that link the sections by:
  - directly comparing one style of art with another
  - indirectly comparing them by mentioning something new
  - discussing where the artworks were created
  - identifying where a new idea replaces an old one
  - identifying linguistic cohesive devices which link sections (e.g. *phrases involving dates, such as "from about"*).
- Once children have compared the sections, make new groups comprising one 'expert' from each of the previous groups. (All children will be experts in their new groups since they will need to represent the ideas from their previous group.) In their new groups, the experts should take it in turns to share their annotation and observations with the rest of the group.

Analysing paragraphs

- Do children remember what topic sentences are? (*The first sentence in a non-fiction paragraph which often summarises the information in the paragraph.*)
  - Ask children to work in pairs and underline the topic sentences.
  - Tell them to read the text, reading only the topic sentences. Do they feel they have a good understanding of what the text covers? Clarify that reading topic sentences is a good way to skim for overall gist, but is not a reliable way of finding information.
  - Remind children that summaries are written in sentences. Model summarising one paragraph. Explain which ideas you leave out and how the final summary brings ideas together succinctly.
  - In their pairs, children should then read each paragraph and write their own summary of its contents.
  - Ask children whether these summaries give more information than the topic sentences.

Stage 3: Analysing the text purpose and language

Activities:

Analysing formality

- All texts are written using a rich range of words, phrases and text features in order that the texts are not too 'samey' and boring to read.
- Ask children to consider whether this text is primarily written:
  - in the first person (look for pronouns *I, me, we, us, mine, ours*)
  - in the second person (look for pronouns *you, yours*)
  - in the third person (look for pronouns *he, she, they, them, theirs*).
- Agree that it's mostly in the third person. Discuss the impact of this decision, considering what kind of text it would be if it were written in the first or second person.
- Ask children whether they think the language of the text is formal or informal.
- Work together to find examples of formal and informal language in the text – particularly of the passive voice. When the children are secure in their understanding of these grammatical terms/features ask them to use agreed colours to identify examples of formal/informal language such as:

Resources needed:

Shared copy of the text (PDF/IWB/visualiser)

Each child needs:
- a copy of the text
- different coloured highlighters/pens/pencils (ideally consistent colours for all children).

Formal language	Informal language
passives (e.g. "*Egypt was ruled by kings, called pharaohs*"), conditionals ("*they would have*") and subjunctives	contractions (*you're, don't*)
longer sentences with more clauses	everyday vocabulary (e.g. *hassle*)
more advanced punctuation (e.g. *semi-colons, colons, dashes, hyphens*)	general verb (*get*) rather than specific verb (*acquired/borrowed*)
vocabulary you might hear on news programmes and documentaries ("*a people*", "*dominated*", "*period*")	incomplete sentences (*Why?*)
	adverbs such as *anyway*
	idioms (e.g. *get things out of your system, goes off in your face*)
generally written in the third person	sentences may start with conjunctions, e.g. *and, but, so, because*

- Discuss the impact on the reader of the level of formality of this text:
  - Does it meet expectations?
  - Does it make you want to read it?
  - Does it make you trust what it says?

Analysing language and sentence structure

- Ask children to work in pairs to identify:
  - conjunctions (e.g. *but, and, so, because, although*)
  - adverbials (e.g. "*During Classical times*"; "*from about 2000 BCE*"; "*particularly on Crete*")
  - prepositions (e.g. "*from Egyptian tomb paintings to Minoan palace decorations*"; "*art flourished on the Greek Islands*"; "*They decorated tombs with images of everyday life*").

  Discuss whether the words are similar to those they would expect in a less formal text.

- Can children remember the signs of a passive construction? (*You can find or insert the words 'by someone' somewhere after the verb; you will see part of the verb 'to be' together with a past participle; the subject of the sentence is not the person doing the action.*) Identify one of the passive constructions in the text (e.g. *"Most early art was [actually] made …"*).

- Ask children to identify passives in the text (e.g. *"Egypt was ruled by kings, called pharaohs"; "Greeks were fascinated by"; "standards they set … have been admired and imitated"; "were influenced by their art"; "wall paintings were lost when buildings were destroyed"*). Discuss why the writer used passives. Discuss possibilities including:
  - she wanted to hide the person/people who did the verb (*unlikely in a non-fiction text*)
  - for brevity; she didn't want to talk about who did the action (*likely*)
  - she wanted to emphasise the outcome of the action rather than the action itself (*likely*).
- Ask children to identify any other sentence which is unlike sentence structures used in speech. Discuss why the author may have chosen to use these structures.

Analysing punctuation

- Check that children recognise and understand the functions of:
  - parentheses (e.g. *to add information which is in addition to the main information in the sentence, and which is not part of the grammatical structure of the main clause; parentheses are usually captured between two commas, brackets or dashes*)
  - dashes (*to emphasise parenthetical information*)
  - hyphens (*to link words together to create a single word*).
- In pairs, ask children to highlight and identify uses of:
  - dashes (e.g. *"from Ancient times – from Egyptian tomb paintings to Minoan palace decorations"*)
  - hyphens (e.g. *"one Egyptian word for sculptor can be translated as 'he-who-keeps-alive'"*)
  - parenthesis (e.g. *"From about 2000 BCE, art flourished on the Greek islands, particularly on Crete, where a people called the Minoans lived"*).

In each case, discuss the impact of the writer's choice of punctuation and explore other punctuation that might have been used instead.

Stage 4: Planning to write: Writing a formal information text

Activities:

- Prior to the session, decide whether you want the children to use the notes on the writing framework or, if you are studying an artist, to link the unit with curriculum work.
- Tell children that they will be planning and writing about art. You expect a text of at least two or three short sections, including a brief introduction, based on the model text.
- Ask children to make notes of useful words they come across in texts about art so that you can create a class word bank.
- Organise children into groups to research an artist or a period in art. Otherwise, the writing framework contains notes about early Asian and Middle Eastern art which children can use to create a text. If children use these notes, emphasise that if they need to invent some appropriate and linked information (e.g. the purpose or subject matter of the artwork), they will not be penalised – the aim is to develop writing style rather than giving accurate facts. You will need to amend the success criteria (online at My Rising Stars) if children are researching different periods.

Resources needed:

Shared copy of the text (PDF/IWB/visualiser)

Access to websites/prospectuses of your school and next school(s)

The success criteria

Each child needs:
- the copy of the text they have previously highlighted and annotated
- the writing framework from page 58 (some children may benefit from this being enlarged to A3).

Cracking Writing Year 6 · Unit 5

- Ask children to:
  - number the sections to show the order in which they will use them
  - write brief headings for each section either for information, or to engage and interest readers.
  - make notes to show the information they plan to use in each section
  - research pictures to illustrate their writing – pictures are important in texts about art, especially unfamiliar art styles – they can either be printed and stuck in place or integrated into electronic texts.
- Discuss the words children noted down, and collect more from the model text. Organise the words into lists, showing synonyms and words that have linked meanings. Explain that all children can use their shared word bank to help them to use some appropriate and formal vocabulary in their writing.
- Briefly, revisit the model text to look at the organisation, links between sections and progression of ideas through the text.
- Model making notes for a section of text.
  - If you are using the writing framework, ask the children to help you to number the points to show the order in which you will use them and to discuss links.
  - If writing about a different artist, model organising your notes to show links between pieces of information.
- Let children work with response partners to discuss, identify and note their own ideas for the content of each section of their text.
- Ask children to swap partners so they can talk through their ideas with new partners.
  - In addition to sharing the notes, children should try talking through some of the ideas in more depth with this new talk partner. Encourage them to annotate the paper with additional ideas, information, vocabulary and phrases. They can also include notes about feedback and suggestions given.
  - Ask children to swap to a third partner to review existing ideas and to try talking through different ideas in more depth. Again encourage them to make annotations.
- Give children time to make improvements based on feedback from response partners.
- Ask the children to discuss what makes a successful formal report/information text on art and use their ideas to clarify and edit the success criteria (online at My Rising Stars).

Stage 5: Writing

Activities:

- Remind children that their task is to write an information text about an artist or art during a specified period. They should base their writing on the model text.
- Model writing a paragraph from the notes you made at the previous stage. Try to include pronouns, conjunctions, adverbials, prepositions, passive voice and parentheses. Use formal language and make use of the list of useful words you created at Stage 4 (above).

Resources needed:

Each child needs:
- the copy of the text they have previously highlighted and annotated
- the completed and annotated writing framework, including the success criteria
- a PC/laptop/tablet if the children are word-processing.

- Give children a few minutes to 'talk like a writer' and tell their partner the text as they plan to write it. If it helps, ask them to use a polite 'writer's voice'.
- Let response partners give some brief feedback before children swap roles.
- Read aloud the success criteria (online at My Rising Stars).
- Let the children write. If children are using IT, remind them to constantly review and edit their writing as they go.
- Throughout the writing session, quietly let the children know how long they have spent, where in their text they should expect to be now and how long there is left.
- Five minutes before the end of the session, ask all children to stop writing and read their text aloud to themselves. If they find errors, missing words or words they can improve, they should use this opportunity to make changes.

Stage 6: Improving, editing, reviewing and sharing the writing

Activities:

- Revisit together the success criteria (online at My Rising Stars).
- Model the process below using your work as an example. The children can give you feedback on each step of the process. After you model a step, the children should have a go with their partner at editing their own work.

Resources needed:

Each child needs:
- the success criteria
- their writing/completed writing framework
- different coloured highlighters/pens.

- Ask children to reread their texts three times with their response partner:
  - First read through: Children read their partner's text out loud to them. The child who wrote the text listens to check that their writing makes sense, listens out for obvious errors and checks the text follows their plan. Children then swap roles.
  - Second read through: Children read their partner's text and highlight the success criteria they have met. They suggest three places where their partner could improve their work (to achieve or further improve on the success criteria).
  - Third read through: Children proofread their partner's text together with them. They check for errors in punctuation and spelling and correct these as necessary. You should give input at this stage if needed.

Lessons from writing

- Prior to the session, identify errors that were commonly made. Write sample sentences that need to be corrected and ask the children to help you to fix them. These could include:
  - informal, instead of formal, language, e.g.
    - *Chinese art is really old and lots of the stuff, like pottery and statues and that, is over 10,000 years old!*
    - Clarify that formality is not referring to the information, which is largely accurate here, but to the style.
    - Challenge children to make the information sound more like a book about art.
  - lack of topic sentences, e.g.
    - *A big city was found which contained huge buildings with stone pillars and marble floors. The pillars were carved with beautiful and realistic images of vultures and foxes.*
    - Ask children to suggest a topic sentence that might contextualise and summarise the information.

Improving the writing

- **After the texts have been marked**: give the children time to read through your comments, to look at the success criteria and to implement any changes suggested. This should not involve the children rewriting the entire report – just those parts that you would like them to revisit to practise/improve their writing. If they have generated their text using IT, you may want them to use a different font/colour for these prompted edits.

Share

Sometimes, children write text to practise writing text. Other times, there is a planned reason or an audience. If you want children to share their writing:

- create an art gallery; this could be a display or a book – ask each child to print a relevant image together with a few paragraphs of text about it
- create a class multimedia display to celebrate the work using images and samples of writing from each child together with a sound track; put the multimedia display on your school/class website.

Unit 5: Writing a formal information text

Name: **Class:** **Date:**

Use either your own research, or the notes given below, for your own report text.

Mesopotamian art (from Ancient Iraq)

- 3200 BCE Uruk city: huge buildings with patterns and mosaics of painted cones
- Sculpture and metal casting including lifelike images of creatures, particularly lions and bulls
- Pictures on clay tablets record trade and pay
- Since 3000 BCE images of horses and camels in sculpture, paintings on clay pots and jewellery

---

Chinese art is divided into periods called after the ruling dynasties.

- Existed for thousands of years
- Pottery and sculpture from around 10,000 BCE
- Early paintings show religious and supernatural beliefs
- Thin brush strokes, in coloured ink, show people, animals and landscapes
- 1200 BCE Terracotta army – thousands of full-sized terracotta soldiers surrounded Emperor's tomb

---

Iranian art

Elam 400–300 BCE

- Images of animals behaving in human ways, linked to myths and fables
- Both natural and abstract images of creatures

Iranian art continued …

- Developments in art parallel those in the west, but generally a couple of centuries earlier
- Influenced by a range of culture and traditions including: Chinese, Indian, Korean, Japanese, Persian and Islamic

---

Turkish art

Göbekli Tepe 1100–800 BCE

- Big city with stone pillars and marble floors
- Pillars carved with images of vultures and foxes
- Wall paintings of animals in homes

Japanese art from around 10,000 BCE

- Influenced by other cultures
- Early paintings showed decorative stick figures
- 1100 BCE scroll paintings – stories from history and legend – lifelike people
- 350 BCE learned how to make bronze – used to spread Buddhist art, and images of Buddha

---

1. Choose an introduction and 2–3 sections to write about.
2. Number the sections to show the order in which you will use them.
3. On the back of this sheet, write headings for each section.
4. Highlight which information you will include – add anything else you know in the margin or on the back of this sheet, and cross out anything you don't intend to use.
5. Research pictures to illustrate your writing.

Unit 5: Moderating writing: Writing a formal information text

Name: Date:

	Text structure and organisation	Text purpose	Sentence structure	Vocabulary and descriptions	Punctuation	Spelling and handwriting
Working at greater depth within the expected standard	Cohesive links between paragraphs enable the reader to compare and contrast information given.	The level of formality is controlled and sometimes manipulated to engage the reader.	Grammatical structures are manipulated to maintain the level of formality.	Technical and subject specific vocabulary used is appropriate and integrated well into text.	A full range of taught punctuation is used, mostly accurately.	Handwriting is effortlessly fast, fluent and easy to read or word-processing is fast, fluent and generally accurate.
	Topic sentences effectively introduce and summarise paragraphs.		Controlled and appropriate use of the passive voice where appropriate is included.		Colons and/or semi-colons are used accurately when used in lists and between clauses.	Spelling – including of less familiar words – is generally accurate.
Working at the expected standard	Ideas are effectively grouped together in paragraphs and show clear progression (e.g. chronological).	Largely formal text presents clear and appropriate information through the choice of specific vocabulary and more complex sentence structures (including passives).	Pronouns, adverbials and prepositional phrases (of time) are used appropriately to aid cohesion between sentences and paragraphs.	Vocabulary is generally appropriate to the level of formality within the text.	Some parenthesis is marked with commas, brackets or dashes.	Most words on the Year 5/6 list – or words of equivalent challenge – are correctly spelled.
					Commas are used for clarity as well as in lists and after fronted adverbials.	Unstressed vowels are generally accurate.
	Headings are used appropriately to engage and inform.		A wide range of clause structures is used, sometimes varying their position within the sentence.	Technical and subject specific vocabulary is used appropriately.	Some use of semi-colons to demonstrate close relationship between clauses is shown.	Legibility, fluency and speed determine which letters are left unjoined.
			At least one appropriate use of the passive voice is included.			Handwriting is easily legible and may be sloped forwards for speed or word-processing is at least as fast as handwriting and often accurate.
Working towards the expected standard	Paragraphs are generally used to organise ideas.	Some evidence of more formal vocabulary and longer sentences is shown.	Pronouns and adverbials are used appropriately to aid cohesion between paragraphs.	Evidence of some technical and subject specific vocabulary being used appropriately is shown.	Apostrophes are consistently used correctly.	Some words on the Year 5/6 list – or words of equivalent challenge – are correctly spelled.
			Fronted adverbials at the beginning of paragraphs indicate a change of time or place.		Commas are used within a series of actions to clarify meaning.	In handwriting, most letters are appropriately joined or word-processing is nearly as fast as handwriting.

Bullies, Bigmouths and So-Called Friends
Jenny Alexander

This is an extract adapted from a book called Bullies, Bigmouths and So-Called Friends *by Jenny Alexander. It offers lots of great advice on how to deal with bullies and build up your confidence in school and at home.*

Prepare to say goodbye to bullies, bigmouths and so-called friends.

Bullies …

You know the type. They push you around, shut doors in your face, send you threatening text messages, take your dinner money, damage your things, mock you and make you feel small.

Bigmouths …

You know the type. They make sarcastic comments about you, spread nasty rumours, and say rude things behind your back.

So-called friends …

Aren't they the worst? They turn their back on you without saying why, tell everyone your secrets, block you on social media and shut you out.

You

Everyone gets hassle from bullies, bigmouths and so-called friends sometimes, but some people handle it better than others.

Talk about it

If you don't want to talk about it, you're probably thinking …

"I should be able to sort this out for myself."

Well, talking is the best way to start! Now you're probably saying …

"But there's nothing anyone else can do!"

That's not the point! The point of talking about it is to make you

- feel better because bad secrets make you uncomfortable and ashamed
- see the situation more clearly because you can't see something you're sitting on
- act more calmly because bottled up feelings are like a shaken-up can of cola – lift the tab and it goes off in your face

The safest way to start is by talking to someone who can't interfere, take over or make you say more than you're ready to. Here are examples of some good talk partners: ChildLine (phone 0800 1111), your rabbit, a picture of your favourite team or singer, a diary or even a friendly tree.

Keep a diary

Keeping a diary, or a picture diary, is a good idea anyway. It helps you get things out of your system and see what's going on more clearly. A diary can also be used as evidence, along with any hurtful text messages and emails, if you decide to tell your parents and teachers.

Five top tips for keeping a diary

1. Use an ordinary notebook, not a proper diary. Then on days when you feel like writing a lot you'll always have enough room, and when you don't feel like writing at all you won't have a gap. And there's always space for pictures if you want to add them.
2. Keep your diary somewhere safe. No one should read it unless you want them to.
3. Write down the facts – dates, times, names and places.
4. Write down how you feel.
5. Be completely honest. Lying to your diary is like lying to yourself.

Five top tips for keeping a picture diary

1. Write the date at the top of a page in an ordinary notebook.
2. Draw yourself. It doesn't have to look like you. If you're feeling grumpy you could draw a hippopotamus, or if you're bright and cheerful you could draw a flower.
3. Put other people in if you want to. They don't have to look like themselves either.
4. Fill in some background with anything that feels right, maybe houses or trees, a street or a desert, a room or a black hole.
5. Add any useful words to remind you of how you felt or what happened.

Unit 6: Bullies, Bigmouths and So-Called Friends

Name: Class: Date:

1. Circle the correct option to complete each sentence below.

   (a) A person who spreads nasty rumours is a …

       bully   bigmouth   so-called friend   real friend

   (b) A person who tells everyone about your secrets and laughs at you is a …

       bully   bigmouth   so-called friend   real friend

   (c) A person who listens to you, stands up for you and makes you stronger is a …

       bully   bigmouth   so-called friend   real friend

   (d) A person who just likes to make others feel small is a …

       bully   bigmouth   so-called friend   real friend

2. How is a friendly tree helpful in managing bullies?

   _____

3. Why is it not good to bottle up your feelings?

   _____

4. List **three** ways in which keeping a diary can help you manage bullies, bigmouths and so-called friends.

   _____

   _____

5. Why are notebooks sometimes better than diaries?

   _____

6. List **two** things that are the same in picture diaries and written diaries, and **two** things that are different.

Same	Different

Cracking Writing Year 6 © Rising Stars UK Ltd 2017. You may photocopy this page.

Unit 6: Writing an informal information and procedural text (instructions)

Warning: this unit is about bullying and may result in disclosures. Follow your school's safeguarding policies and procedures. Whilst the information given in this unit can stand alone, it is most usefully taught in the context of personal safety work, particularly as children prepare for transition to secondary school.

In this unit children will:

- read an informal information and instructional text
- consider organisation, headings and topic sentences
- identify the purpose of different parts of the text, comparing language and sentence structures used
- explore features of informal texts
- plan, draft, edit and improve an informal information and instructional text.

Stage 1: Responding to the text

Activities:

- What do the children know about bullying? Work together towards a definition in the children's words. Consider:
  - How is it different from being unkind or falling out? (*Bullying is repetitive and intentionally aims to hurt. One person must have some kind of real or imagined power over the other.*)
  - Does it have to involve physical aggression? (*No.*) Does it usually? (*No.*)
  - What does it feel like to be the victim of a bully? (E.g. *defeated, powerless, useless.*)
  - What does it feel like to be a bully? (E.g. *strong, powerful, sometimes popular, sometimes scary, sometimes like getting revenge for something an adult has done to them.*)

  (The Anti-bullying Alliance (www.anti-bullyingalliance.org.uk) defines bullying as: *The repetitive, intentional hurting of one person or group by another person or group, where the relationship involves an imbalance of power.*)

- *Think, pair, share:* Discuss different forms of and reasons for bullying (e.g. *physical, verbal, social bullying, cyber bullying – including sexting and blackmail; for reasons such as: age, religion, body shape, gender, sexual orientation, social circumstances, SEN or disability*).
- Read the text together:
  - Do the children recognise the distinction between bullies, bigmouths and so-called friends?
- Ensure the children understand the idiomatic language used in the text, e.g. *"get things out of your system"*, *"goes off in your face"*. Explain the meaning of words/phrases where necessary.
- Let children answer the reading comprehension questions to ensure close reading of the text and good understanding.
- Together, share answers to the questions and discuss the strategies children used to answer them.

Resources needed:

Shared copy of the text (PDF/IWB/visualiser)

Each child needs:

- a copy of the text
- a copy of the comprehension questions.

Cracking Writing Year 6 · Unit 6

Stage 2: Analysing the text structure and organisation

Activities:

- Ask children to read the text aloud to a response partner to revisit the text, develop fluency, ensure appropriate pronunciation of all words and to practise reading with good intonation and expression.
- Ask children to underline any new words or phrases. Take feedback and explain what these mean in context.

Resources needed:

Shared copy of the text (PDF/IWB/visualiser)

Each pair needs:
- sticky notes

Each child needs:
- a copy of the text
- highlighters/pens/pencils.

Analysing text structure

- Together, identify the three main headings and ask children to write 1, 2 or 3 at the beginning of each section:
  1. *Prepare to say goodbye to bullies, bigmouths and so-called friends*
  2. *Talk about it*
  3. *Keep a diary.*
- *Think, pair, share:* Discuss how these sections are organised. Ask children to consider the progression of the argument through each section (e.g. *Section 1 introduces the three classes of bullies; Section 2 begins by explaining why it's important to talk about being bullied and then gives ideas about how to talk; Section 3 briefly introduces reasons for keeping diaries and then gives 'top tips' for keeping them*).

Analysing topic sentences

- Discuss the paragraphs. Why are there so many short paragraphs? What is their impact?
- Ask children to work in pairs to:
  - underline the topic sentences (the first sentence in each paragraph)
  - rate the topic sentences as indicative of the paragraph contents; tell children to rate each topic sentence on the basis of:
    - 3 marks = good and useful indication of paragraph contents
    - 2 marks = some indication of paragraph contents
    - 1 mark = little or no useful indication of paragraph contents.

    Tell children to write their marks in the margins.
- Give children the opportunity to move around the class and look at how others have rated the topic sentences. If someone has a different mark, ask them to discuss the differences. They can then decide whether they want to change their mark.
- Model improving one of the topic sentences. Discuss what is wrong with the existing sentence before starting to edit and improve it – or to begin a new topic sentence to put in front of the one from the text.
- In their pairs, ask children to find their lowest-marked topic sentence.
  - Ask them to write three better alternative topic sentences on separate sticky notes and to stick them beside the text.
  - Children should go and look at each other's suggested topic sentences, initialling the best of the three they read for each pair.
  - Children should cross out the less-than-useful topic sentence and replace it with the sentence they wrote that had the highest approval rating.

Cracking Writing Year 6 · Unit 6

Stage 3: Analysing the text purpose and language 📖

Activities:

Discussing text purpose

- Ask groups of children to reread the text aloud to each other and decide initially whether it is fiction or non-fiction (*non-fiction*) and then the purpose of the text (*to help children to develop strategies for dealing with bullying as well as other unkind things people say and do*).

Resources needed:

Shared copy of the text (PDF/IWB/visualiser)

Each child needs:
- a copy of the text
- different coloured pens/pencils (ideally consistent colours for all children).

- Ask children what the difference is between information (e.g. *facts given about something*), advice (e.g. *recommendation as to the best choice to make*) and instructions (e.g. *information about how something should be done*). Write the children's definitions. Together, identify an example of each kind of text and compare it to the definition.
- Working in small groups, ask children to decide what each paragraph is trying to do and to circle it in an agreed colour. Tell them to consider whether each paragraph is mostly giving:
  - information
  - advice
  - instructions.

  Clarify that for some of the paragraphs, there could be more than one answer, but that you want them to decide what they think and be prepared to say why.

Comparing language for instructions and information

- Can children tell you what a command is? (*An instruction.*) Ask which part of speech commands like *Be quiet!* begin with (*an imperative verb, also known as command verb in younger years to emphasise the link to commands*). Can children give more examples of imperative verbs? (E.g. *Put, Make, Wait, Stir, Stand, Do*, etc.)
  - Ask children which kind of text type they associate with imperative verbs (*instructions*).
  - Ask whether imperative verbs always have to be at the beginning of sentences (*no, they can follow adverbs, e.g. Next, make a …*).
  - Model finding an imperative verb in the text (e.g. *"Prepare"* in the first heading).
  - Identify features of the verb which helped you to recognise it (e.g. *It is at the beginning of a sentence; it doesn't have a pronoun or noun with it; it's a second person verb form – i.e. linked with second person pronoun 'You' – so it directly addresses the reader/listener*).
- Ask children to look carefully at the information/advice/instructions paragraphs and to look at what makes the language of each distinctive. Ask them to look for examples of:
  - bullet points in information/advice
  - lists in information/advice
  - imperative verbs in instructions (e.g. *"use", "write", "draw", "put"*, etc.)
  - numbered ideas in instructions.
- Talk about why the author chose to mix text types and purposes in this one short text (e.g. *to keep the reader interested; to allow more efficient sharing of ideas; to allow the reader to scan for text they want to read*).

Analysing formality

- All texts are written using a rich range of words, phrases and text features in order that the texts are not too 'samey' and boring to read.
- Ask children to consider whether this text is primarily written:
  - in the first person (look for pronouns *I, me, we, us, mine, ours*)
  - in the second person (look for pronouns *you, yours*)
  - in the third person (look for pronouns *he, she, they, them, theirs*).

Cracking Writing Year 6 · Unit 6

- Agree that it's mostly in the second person – which matches the use of imperative verbs.
- Discuss the impact of this decision. (*It sounds like it is talking and giving advice and instructions directly to the reader.*)
- Revisit features of some sentence types only found in formal texts such as:
  - passives – look for the verb *to be* followed by a past participle and sentences where the subject isn't doing the action (e.g. *it is said that*)
  - conditionals – look for modal verbs such as *could, would, should* which express the likelihood of something happening (e.g. *I should be able to do this*.)
  - subjunctives – look for *that* followed by the infinitive without *to* (e.g. *I ask that you be honest*) or *were* in contexts like *If I were you …; If you were sensible …*
- Do children expect to find examples of this kind of language in this text? (*No – although there are two conditional "should"s*) Can they explain their answer? (*It is mostly an informal text.*)
- Ask children to use agreed colours to identify examples of formal/informal text such as:

Formal language	Informal language
More complex sentences which may include passives (e.g. *it is said that*), conditionals (e.g. *it may be that*) and subjunctives (e.g. *were you to …*)	More speechlike
Longer sentences with more clauses	Contractions (e.g. *you're, don't*)
More advanced punctuation (e.g. *semi-colons, colons, dashes, hyphens*)	Everyday vocabulary (e.g. *hassle*)
Vocabulary you might hear on news programmes and documentaries (*evidence, confidence*)	General verb (*get*) rather than specific verb (*acquired/borrowed*)
Generally written in the third person	Incomplete sentences
	Adverbs such as *anyway*
	Idioms (e.g. *"get things out of your system"; "goes off in your face"*)
	Humour (e.g. *"draw a hippopotamus"*)
	Sentences may start with conjunctions
	May be in the second person

- Discuss the impact on the reader of the informality of this text.
  - Does it make the text more or less useful to the reader? Why?
  - Does it make the information and ideas seem more or less useful? Why?

Stage 4: Planning to write: Writing an informal information and procedural text (instructions)

Activities:

- Tell children that they are going to write a text about helping children with the move to secondary school (or a new class if appropriate for your school).
- Ask groups of children to create a mind map and record words and phrases to identify things they think they/their friends/their siblings were/are/will be worried about in terms of school/class transition.
- Share ideas to create a class mind map showing common threads in the children's ideas.

Resources needed:

Shared copy of the text (PDF/IWB/visualiser)

Access to websites/prospectuses of your school and next school(s)

The success criteria

Each child needs:
- the copy of the text they have previously highlighted and annotated
- the writing framework from page 69 (some children may benefit from this being enlarged to A3).

- Distribute the writing framework. Model using some of the ideas from the mind map to populate the columns and talk about how you might address the ideas in different ways.
- Ask children to work in pairs to discuss the ideas they will include – this can include some of the suggestions on the writing framework, but should also include ideas from their mind maps.
  - Children should decide whether they will include the ideas as information, advice or instructions.
  - The writing framework should only include labels as reminders of ideas; it is not necessary to write anything out in full.
- Ask children to swap partners so they can talk through their ideas with new partners.
  - In addition to sharing the notes, children should try talking through some of the ideas in more depth with this new talk partner. Encourage them to annotate the writing framework with additional ideas, information, vocabulary and phrases. They can also include notes about feedback and suggestions given.
- Ask children to swap to a third partner to review existing ideas and to try talking through different ideas in more depth. Again, encourage them to make annotations.
- On the reverse of the writing framework, ask children to list the headings they plan to use in the order in which they plan to use them.
- Ask the children to discuss what makes a successful informal text giving advice, information and instructions, and use their ideas to clarify and edit the success criteria (online at My Rising Stars).

Stage 5: Writing

Activities:

- Remind children that their task is to write a text giving information, advice and instructions to help others with the transition to Year 7.
- Write some short model paragraphs using some of the ideas and styles from the plan you made at the previous stage. Try to ensure that you demonstrate using imperative verbs as well as pronouns, conjunctions, adverbs, prepositions and parentheses. Talk to the children about your choice of vocabulary and sentence structure.
- Give children a few minutes to 'talk like a writer' and tell their partner the text as they plan to write it. If it helps, ask them to use a polite 'writer's voice'.
- Let response partners give some brief feedback before children swap roles.
- Read aloud the success criteria (online at My Rising Stars).
- Let the children write. If children are using IT, remind them to constantly review and edit their writing as they go.
- Throughout the writing session, quietly let the children know how long they have spent, where in their text they should expect to be now and how long there is left.
- Five minutes before the end of the session, ask all children to stop writing and read their text aloud to themselves. If they find errors, missing words or words they can improve, they should use this opportunity to make changes.

Resources needed:

Each child needs:
- the copy of the text they have previously highlighted and annotated
- the completed and annotated writing framework, including success criteria
- a PC/laptop/tablet if the children are word-processing.

Cracking Writing Year 6 · Unit 6

Stage 6: Improving, editing, reviewing and sharing the writing

Activities:

- Revisit together the success criteria (online at My Rising Stars).
- Model the process below using your work as an example. The children can give you feedback on each step of the process. After you model a step, the children should have a go with their partner at editing their own work.

Resources needed:

Each child needs:
- the success criteria
- their writing/completed writing framework
- different coloured highlighters/pens.

- Ask children to reread their texts three times with their response partner:
  - First read through: Children read their partner's text out loud to them. The child who wrote the text listens to check that their writing makes sense, listens out for obvious errors and checks the text follows their plan. Children then swap roles.
  - Second read through: Children read their partner's text and highlight the success criteria they have met. They suggest three places where their partner could improve their work (to achieve or further improve on the success criteria).
  - Third read through: Children proofread their partner's text together with them. They check for errors in punctuation and spelling and correct these as necessary. You should give input at this stage if needed.

Lessons from writing

- Prior to the session, identify errors that were commonly made. Write sample sentences that need to be corrected and ask the children to help you to fix them. These could include:
  - confusing pronouns, e.g.
    - *You remember to take the things in your bag and carry it from lesson to lesson.*
    - Pronouns are important for text cohesion – they allow you to follow ideas through the text, but only if they are used consistently. Can children help to organise the pronouns in a sentence such as the one above (remembering that the imperative verb doesn't need a pronoun – it is already in the second person).
  - not punctuating parenthetical information, e.g.
    - *It is better to walk to school with friends who you can call for on the way to school because it makes you more confident when you get there.*
    - Explore the choice of punctuation to mark parentheses, depending on how important it is, and discuss why it is helpful to the reader to know which information is in the main clause and which is an aside.

Improving the writing

- **After the texts have been marked**: give the children time to read through your comments, to look at the success criteria and to implement any changes suggested. This should not involve the children rewriting the entire recount – just those parts that you would like them to revisit to practise/improve their writing. If they have generated their text using IT, you may want them to use a different font/colour for these prompted edits.

Share

Sometimes, children write text to practise writing text. Other times, there is a planned reason or an audience. If you want children to share their writing:

- suggest they work in groups to select parts of each other's texts to use in a transition guide for future year groups
- if the text is already on the computer, ask children to save another version and this time edit it to make it formal – as if the school/Year 7 lead teacher is writing the guide for their new pupils
- let them prioritise their ideas and ask them to create posters to improve transition for other children who will be attending the same secondary school.

Unit 6: Writing an informal information and procedural text (instructions)

Name:　　　　　　　　　　　　　　　　Class:　　　　Date:

List ideas of topics you think it would be helpful to cover in a guide preparing for Year 7. Below are some ideas to get you started, but you should also add your own ideas to the back of this sheet.

- Walk to school with friends
- How to use a homework planner
- Use a map of the site
- Talk to other people before you go
- Open evenings and 'Meet the Tutor' events
- Use the school's website
- Prepare ways of making sure you have what you need when you need it
- Make lists of things you want to remember
- Find out what happens at dinner times and where you can eat

Sort the ideas you want to include into the different columns below to show how you will address them in your text.

Information	Advice	Instructions

Unit 6: Moderating writing: Writing an informal information and procedural text (instructions)

Name: Date:

	Text structure and organisation	Text purpose	Sentence structure	Vocabulary and descriptions	Punctuation	Spelling and handwriting
Working at greater depth within the expected standard	The level of formality of different parts of the text is reflected in paragraph structure.	Controlled length of sections, and appropriate use of different text purposes, makes the text interesting, appealing and appropriate to the reader.	Grammatical structures are manipulated to maintain/change the level of formality.	Vocabulary is manipulated to maintain/change the level of formality.	A full range of taught punctuation is used, mostly accurately.	Handwriting is effortlessly fast, fluent and easy to read.
	Topic sentences effectively introduce and summarise paragraphs.				Colons and/or semi-colons are used accurately.	Spelling – including of less familiar words – is generally accurate.
Working at the expected standard	Paragraphs are used effectively to progress sequence of ideas through the text.	Different purposes of different parts of the text are signalled through appropriate text features and language structures such as use of imperative verbs in commands, and speechlike constructions such as contractions, incomplete sentences, idioms, everyday vocabulary, etc.	Pronouns, adverbials and prepositional phrases are used appropriately to aid cohesion between sentences and paragraphs.	Vocabulary is generally appropriate to the level of formality within the text.	Some parentheses are marked with commas, brackets or dashes.	Most words on the Year 5/6 list – or words of equivalent challenge – are correctly spelled.
					Commas are used for clarity as well as in lists and after fronted adverbials.	Unstressed vowels are generally accurate.
	Headings are used appropriately to continue the style of the model text.		A wide range of clause structures is used, sometimes varying their position within the sentence.	Adverbs and prepositional phrases in expanded noun phrases add detail and precision.	Largely correct use of inverted commas and associated punctuation is shown.	Legibility, fluency and speed determine which letters are left unjoined.
			Use of imperative verbs to form commands is included.			Handwriting is easily legible and may be sloped forwards for speed.
Working towards the expected standard	Paragraphs are generally used to organise ideas.	The overall purpose of the text is evident in the advice and information offered.	Pronouns and adverbials are used appropriately to aid cohesion between paragraphs.	Everyday vocabulary is sometimes used to create informality.	Apostrophes are consistently used correctly.	Some words on the Year 5/6 list – or words of equivalent challenge – are correctly spelled.
	Events are told in a coherent sequence.		Fronted adverbials at the beginning of paragraphs indicate a change of time or place.	Some noun phrases are extended with adjectives and prepositional phrases.	Commas are used within a series of actions to clarify meaning.	In handwriting, most letters are appropriately joined.

Cracking Writing Year 6 © Rising Stars UK Ltd 2017. You may photocopy this page.

The Vanishing Rainforest

Richard Platt

> *The Vanishing Rainforest contains two texts with the same message. The first is a story about the Yanomami tribe who live in the Amazon rainforest. You can read the beginning of the story, together with the non-fiction text.*

The Vanishing Rainforest

Remaema walked lazily through the rainforest towards the river, sucking her favourite wild berries. At the water's edge, she washed her sticky hands. The muddy water hurried past her to join the world's largest river – the Amazon.

Remaema heard a noise. It sounded like an insect close to her ear, but it came from the distant river bank. When the buzzing stopped, the tree-tops moved and one of the tallest trees fell.

She hurried home and told her mother what she had seen. "Child, it is the *nabë*. You heard the machine they use to cut trees."

Remaema nodded. The nabë were white people – strangers. They had come to take away her forest.

As the sun set, Remaema's uncle Moawa returned to the *yano* – the round house which all the families shared. He proudly carried a new *machete*, and wore a red T-shirt.

Remaema's father asked where he got such precious things.

"From the nabë," he replied.

"Brother, you are helping the nabë who are cutting down our trees?"

"These people are powerful …!" Moawa replied angrily. "They have guns. They can kill us before we get close enough to hit them with an arrow. If we give them what they want, they will reward us. If we don't help them, they will take it anyway."

Then everyone spoke at once and started arguing.

"STOP!"

Her grandfather's shout made Remaema jump. Everyone went quiet. "I have travelled far, and I have seen the nabë cutting down trees, destroying our world. If we help them, we make our own ruin."

Moawa defended himself, "The forest will return: we make clearings, too, for growing bananas and *cassava*. When we move on, trees soon cover our gardens …"

"No!" The old man stopped him. "We make small clearings. But when the nabë come, they take away every tree. When all the trees have gone, the animals die. It is the animals that spread the seeds of the trees. No animals, no forest. No forest, no food. Then we will all starve."

Remaema's grandfather was right. To grow their plants, the farmers cut down trees and set fire to the forest. They soon moved on, but the trees did not grow back.

The fires scared away the forest animals. Peccaries used to be common once, but after the nabë came, hunters no longer caught these tasty forest pigs. Many fruit trees had vanished too. Finding enough food took much longer. Sometimes there was nothing at all.

The nabë needed the help of guides such as Moawa. They offered tools, clothes and money in exchange. But afterwards, the farmers only paid the guides half what they had promised. Villagers tried to hunt down the nabë who had cheated them, but the farmers kept them away with their guns.

Then, Remaema met a nabë who was not like the others. She was washing when the sound of a motor boat drifted upriver. Remaema watched from the forest shadows. A young woman began unloading. Remaema started to creep away.

"Wait! Don't go!" To her surprise, Remaema could understand the tall, blond woman's word.

"Take this …" The woman held out a shiny square. It reflected Remaema's face like a puddle, only brighter. "My name is Jane."

Why Rainforests Matter

Rainforests once ringed the world like a belt. They covered much of the wettest land around the Earth's middle. The forests are shrinking fast. Nearly half have gone because people cut trees wastefully for timber or to make paper. Every second, timber workers cut down an area of rainforest as big as 16 tennis courts.

Jane, the scientist in the story, knows that we must preserve the rainforest because of the huge variety of useful and beautiful plants and animals that live there. For each kind of rainforest plant that scientists have found and named, there may be as many as six more yet to be discovered. Forest people are the only ones who know how to make food or healing drugs from these plants. Some South American groups use as many as 1300 different plants.

But there is another reason for preserving the world's greatest rainforests. They control our planet's climate, its weather pattern. The trees soak up waste gases that pollute the atmosphere. Cutting down the trees frees the gases. This changes the climate, making it hotter and stormier.

By preserving the rainforests and the plants, people and other animals they contain, we are safeguarding our own health – and the health of our planet.

Unit 7: The Vanishing Rainforest

Name: Class: Date:

1. Find and copy **two** facts you learn about Remaema's home in the first paragraph.

   _____

   _____

2. Do you agree with Moawa's attitude to the nabë? Explain your answer, using evidence from the text.

   _____

   _____

3. If it's OK for the Yanomami people to make small clearings, why is it *not* OK for the nabë to make bigger clearings?

   _____

4. Why is the forest shrinking fast?

   _____

5. Give **two** reasons from the text why we need to save the rainforests.

   _____

   _____

6. Using information from the text, tick **one** or **two** boxes in each row to show which messages are in each of the texts.

Message	Fiction	Non-fiction
Rainforests are being cut down.		
The Yanomami people can't live without the rainforest.		
Some plants in the rainforests can be used to cure disease.		
The rainforests help to control the Earth's climate.		
All the trees, plants, creatures and insects must be saved together – it's no use just saving some of them.		

Cracking Writing Year 6 · Unit 7

Unit 7 Writing a biased text and story with the same message

In this unit children will:
- read a biased text and story which contain the same message and consider the organisation of these texts
- compare and contrast the features and language structures of the text types
- identify cohesive devices and persuasive techniques
- consider punctuation and its impact
- plan, draft, edit and improve a biased text and story with the same message.

Stage 1: Responding to the text

Activities:

- *Think, pair, share:* Ask children to jot down notes about the rainforest.
  - What do they know about it?
  - Where are rainforests? (*Near the equator in South America, Africa, South East Asia, Australia.*)
  - Who/what lives/grows there? (*Trees, plants, insects, animals, people …*) Why are they under threat? (*Timber; pasture for cattle; planting commercial crops such as avocados, bananas, pineapples, tea, coffee; mining for valuable minerals and metals; oil exploration; dams.*)
  - Why does it matter? (*Loss of habitat for creatures and home for indigenous peoples; potential for medicine and useful foods; climate control and greenhouse gases; prevention of flooding.*)
- Create a whole class chart recording children's prior knowledge and understanding of issues surrounding threats to rainforests.
- Before you read the text together, explain that it contains two different text types: the first is the beginning of a story and the second is an information report that has a clear bias.
- Explain the meaning of words from the text that the children may not have come across before, e.g. *"machete"*, *"cassava"*, *"safeguarding"*, *"atmosphere"*, *"preserving"* and *"climate"*.
- Read the text together and discuss:
  - Are the concerns in the texts similar to the ones the children have already identified?
  - What have they learned from these texts?
  - Can they identify the bias in the writing? What is the message the author wants readers to understand?
- Ask the children to answer the reading comprehension questions to ensure close reading of the text and good understanding.
- Together, share answers to the questions and discuss the strategies children used to answer them.

Resources needed:

Shared copy of the text (PDF/IWB/visualiser)
Flipchart/large paper
Each child needs:
- a copy of the text
- a copy of the comprehension questions.

Stage 2: Analysing the text structure and organisation

Activities:

- Ask children to read the text aloud to a response partner to revisit the text, develop fluency, ensure appropriate pronunciation of all words and to practise reading with good intonation and expression.
- Ask children to underline any new words or phrases. Take feedback and explain what these mean in context.

Resources needed:

Shared copy of the text (PDF/IWB/visualiser)

Each child needs:
- a copy of the text
- highlighters/coloured pencils.

Identifying cohesive devices

- Ask children to consider what determines the sequence and progression of ideas in each text. (*Fiction: chronology – shows the order of events. Non-fiction: grouping of ideas to flow through the argument. Paragraph 1 sets out the big picture; paragraph 2 introduces the main argument about people's health; paragraph 3 adds another argument about the planet's health; paragraph 4 joins together information from previous paragraphs.*)
- Ask children what they understand by the term 'cohesion' when discussing texts, e.g. *A text has cohesion if it is clear how the meanings of its parts fit together.* Cohesive devices that can help to do this include:
  - *determiners and pronouns* – which refer back to previous words
  - *conjunctions and adverbs* – which make relationships between ideas clear
  - *referral to things previously mentioned*.
- Work with children to identify examples of each cohesive device as a class before they work in their groups.
- Organise children into groups. Ask each group to focus on either the fiction or the non-fiction text and:
  - highlight/list cohesive devices (*determiners, pronouns, adverbials, prepositional phrases, conjunctions*) used to make links between identified ideas
  - identify ways in which topic and context are linked through the text
  - list technical vocabulary that helps to identify the topic or setting.
- Ask nominated 'experts' from each group to report back to the class on the words and ideas they listed.

Comparing texts

- Ask children to draw a table with three columns headed: 'Fiction', 'Non-fiction' and 'Same/different'.
- Working in pairs, ask children to identify up to five text features (sentence features will be addressed at Stage 3) to comment on for each of the texts, and then to observe whether they are the same or different, e.g.

Fiction	Non-fiction	Same/different
Topic is the rainforest	Topic is the rainforest	Same
Story with characters, plot, etc.	Facts only	Different
Characters have names	No names are used	Different
Scientists want to learn about medicines from rainforest people	Scientists want to learn about medicines from rainforest people	Same
Organised chronologically	Organised to join together ideas	Different
Uses dialogue	No dialogue	Different
Contains true information/facts	Contains true information/facts	Same
Wants to educate and persuade people about rainforest destruction	Wants to educate and persuade people about rainforest destruction	Same

Cracking Writing Year 6 · Unit 7

Stage 3: Analysing the text purpose and language

Activities:

Comparing text purpose

- Ask pairs of children to reread the texts aloud to each other and decide *how* they know that one is fiction and one is non-fiction. Expect answers like:
  - *In the fiction, characters have names and relationships.*
  - *Only the fiction has dialogue and description.*
  - *The fiction is organised chronologically, to list the events, and so paragraphs start with adverbials.*
- Ask children to consider the purpose of each of these texts.
  - Why did the author write a story on this topic? (*To education/inform/persuade.*)
  - What does he want the reader's response to be? (*Sympathetic to his cause.*)
  - Is the purpose of the texts the same or different? (*Overall, it's the same.*)
- Discuss the impact of persuasion through a story versus facts. Ask children in the class which approach they prefer. Clarify that different approaches work for different people.

Resources needed:

Shared copy of the text (PDF/IWB/visualiser)

Each child needs:
- the copy of the text
- coloured pens/pencils/markers.

Considering persuasive techniques

- Ask children to work in pairs to identify how the texts try to achieve their persuasive purpose. Invite children to explore a whole range of techniques they observe. Work together to identify features such as:
  - emotive statements (e.g. *"They had come to take away her forest"*; *"No animals, no forest. No forest, no food. Then we will all starve"*; *"save the forest"*; *"destroying our world"*; *"If we help them, we make our own ruin."*; *"These people are powerful …!"*; *"useful and beautiful plants and animals"*)
  - emotive words (**verbs:** *"destroying"*, *"starve"*, *"die"*, *"shrinking"*, *"preserve"*, *"save"*, *"discovered"*, *"control"*, *"soak up"*, *"pollute"*; **nouns:** *"ruin"*, *"strangers"*; **adjectives:** *"precious"*, *"powerful"*, *"greatest"*, *"safeguarding"*; **adverbs:** *"wastefully"*)
  - information which is included and which is not included, e.g. snakes, spiders, biting insects, poisonous plants are not mentioned but *"useful and beautiful plants and animals"* are
  - giving the nabè a name which emphasises how alien they are
  - using *"our"* in the final paragraph of non-fiction to make the reader feel involved.
- Discuss other persuasive techniques the children observed.

Comparing language and sentence structure

- Ask children to focus on the types of sentences and the language used in the different texts. Add the new information to the table started at Stage 2 (above). They may observe, e.g.

Fiction	Non-fiction	Same/different
Some paragraphs often start with adverbials	Paragraphs start with topic sentences	Different
Some description using adjectives and adverbs	Some description using adjectives	Same/different
Past tense	Present tense	Different
Uses dialogue	No dialogue	Different
Uses ellipses to show incomplete ideas	All sentences and ideas are complete	Different
Uses first, second and third person pronouns	Mostly third person pronouns	Different
Most sentences begin with determiners, noun phrases or pronouns Other ways of starting sentences include: adverbs and adverbials (*"When we move on"*, *"then"*, *"when the buzzing stopped"*, *"As the sun set"*), conjunctions (*"if"*, *"but"*), verbs (*"Wait"*, *"Don't"*, *"Take"*)	Comparatively few sentences begin with pronouns or nouns but there are some expanded noun phrases (*"Every second"*, *"Some South American"*) Sentences begin with prepositions (*"By"*) conjunctions (*"For"*, *"But"*) and adverbs (*"now"*, *"nearly"*)	Different

- Talk about the impact of these language choices.
- Point out that there are more differences in the language and sentences structures of the fiction and non-fiction texts than there are in the contents.

Analysing punctuation

- As you seek and identify each punctuation mark, explain its use and purpose as illustrated in this text. In pairs, ask children to highlight and identify uses of:
  - colons (*"The forest will return: we make clearings, too, for growing bananas and cassava."*)
  - dashes (*"the world's largest river – the Amazon"*; *"white people – strangers"*; *"yano – the round house"*; *"we are safeguarding our own health – and the health of our planet"*)
  - hyphens (*"the tree-tops"*; *"t-shirt"*)
  - parentheses (*"Now, however, the forests"*, *"Scientists, like Jane in the story, know"*)
  - ellipses (*"cover our gardens …"*; *"Take this …"*).
- Ask children to identify reasons why:
  - ellipses are only used in the narrative
    - Discuss where they are used.
  - most of the other, more advanced, punctuation is only in the non-fiction
    - Discuss why this should be so and look carefully at where it is used.
- Together, identify commas used in both texts and discuss their use. Then, in pairs or groups of three, ask children to highlight all commas and then to list all the different uses for commas they can find in the text.

Cracking Writing Year 6 · Unit 7

Stage 4: Planning to write: Writing a biased text and story with the same message

Activities:

- Prior to the session, identify the topic you would like children to write about in both a story and a non-fiction text. Look for a persuasive topic that is linked to a curriculum area you are exploring, or to something that is in the news and accessible to children. You may want to amend the success criteria to reflect the topics.
- Explain to the children that you want them to write a story and a biased text which both have the same message. Tell them the topic you have selected.
- If there is time, allocate different positions to groups of children and give them the opportunity to prepare to debate the topic. They will learn about 'pro' and 'con' arguments by listening to each other.
- In groups, ask children to discuss the topic under consideration, between them finding as many reasons both 'for' and 'against' the proposal as they can. Ask scribes for each group to record the ideas on a large sheet of paper.
- Introduce the writing framework. Explain that there will not be room for all of the children's ideas in the text they will write, so they should select the most powerful and persuasive ideas. Remind them that the ideas must be linked so they can be expressed in a short story as well as a piece of biased text. Model recording one of three key points and a summary statement, and talk together about how these could be woven into a story.
- Ask children to work in pairs with the writing framework. It is easier if both children in a pair plan to adopt the same approach to the subject.
  - Ask children to complete the writing framework for the non-fiction text first, identifying the most powerful, compelling reasons for their stance. On the writing framework, they should list:
    - notes for up to three key points and a summary statement
    - possible topic sentences or paragraph beginnings
    - thematic links through paragraphs
    - useful vocabulary.
  - Once they have identified the points they plan to make, ask children to begin to plan a story outline which makes the same persuasive point, but illustrates it through a story. Before children record anything, they should have discussed and agreed on the story outline.
  - Then they should record:
    - a story problem, action, resolution and conclusion
    - ideas for starting paragraphs
    - story links through paragraphs
    - useful vocabulary.
- Briefly, revisit the model texts to explore ideas to 'borrow' about:
  - ways ideas are linked
  - text organisation and structure of paragraphs
  - establishing place and people
  - use of dialogue
  - paragraph openings
  - language, tense, pronouns, punctuation, sentence beginnings.

Resources needed:

Shared copy of the text (PDF/IWB/visualiser)
The success criteria
Access to websites
Each group needs:
- large paper

Each child needs:
- the copy of the text they have previously highlighted and annotated
- the writing framework from page 81 (some children may benefit from this being enlarged to A3).

- Ask children to swap partners so they can talk through their ideas with new partners.
  - In addition to sharing the notes, children should try talking through some of the ideas in more depth with this new talk partner. Encourage them to annotate the paper with additional ideas, information, vocabulary and phrases. They can also include notes about feedback and suggestions given.
  - Ask children to swap to a third partner to review existing ideas, and to try talking through different ideas in more depth. Again encourage them to make annotations.
- Give children time to make improvements based on feedback from response partners.
- Ask the children to discuss success criteria that would be suitable for both of the texts. Use their ideas to clarify and edit the success criteria (online at My Rising Stars).

Stage 5: Writing

Activities:

- Remind children that their task is to write two texts with the same persuasive message: one fiction, one non-fiction. Allow children to write the texts separately, ideally on separate occasions.
- Model writing opening paragraphs for each of the texts, using the planning notes you made at Stage 4. Ensure that your paragraphs are different in tone, to reflect narrative/non-narrative and try to include: persuasive and emotive language which is specific and relevant to the topic, a range of clause structures, a different range of pronouns in each text, cohesive devices including different ways of beginning sentences and a variety of ways of using commas.
- Give children a few minutes to 'talk like a writer' and tell their partner what they plan to write in each of the texts. If it helps, ask them to use a polite 'writer's voice'.
- Let response partners give some brief feedback before children swap roles.
- Read aloud the success criteria (online at My Rising Stars).
- Let the children write. If children are using IT, remind them to constantly review and edit their writing as they go.
- Throughout the writing session, quietly let the children know how long they have spent, where in their text they should expect to be now and how long there is left.
- Five minutes before the end of the session, ask all children to stop writing and read their text aloud to themselves. If they find errors, or missing words or words they can improve, they should use this opportunity to make changes.

Resources needed:

The success criteria
Each child needs:
- the copy of the text they have previously annotated
- the completed and annotated writing framework, including the success criteria
- a PC/laptop/tablet if the children are word-processing.

Stage 6: Improving, editing, reviewing and sharing the writing

Activities:

- Revisit together the success criteria (online at My Rising Stars).
- Model the process below using your work as an example. It will be easier for the children to learn if you deal with each text separately. The children can give you feedback on each step of the process. After you model a step the children should have a go with their partner at editing their own work.
- Ask children to reread their texts three times with their response partner:
  - First read through: Children read their partner's text out loud to them. The child who wrote the text listens to check that their writing makes sense, listens out for obvious errors and checks the text follows their plan. Children then swap roles.

Resources needed:

Each child needs:
- the success criteria
- their writing/completed writing framework
- different coloured highlighters/pens.

Cracking Writing Year 6 · Unit 7

- Second read through: Children read their partner's text and highlight the success criteria they have met. They suggest three places where their partner could improve their work (to achieve or further improve on the success criteria).
- Third read through: Children proofread their partner's text together with them. They check for errors in punctuation and spelling and correct these as necessary. You should give input at this stage if needed.

Lessons from writing

- Prior to the session, identify errors that were commonly made. Write sample sentences that need to be corrected and ask the children to help you to fix them. These could include:
  - confusing pronouns, e.g.
    - *Dad said we had to hurry but Hari couldn't hurry because he was too hungry. He picked him up and put him on his back.*
    - Sentences like this are confusing for the reader and don't help with cohesion. Ask children how they would clarify the text and why they would make those choices.
  - inaccurate use of commas, e.g.
    - *For Maria the trek, along the railway line was endless. She stumbled on her short tired legs as she tried to keep up with the others. The burden, she carried on her back, was heavy but, there was no time to rest.*
    - Clarify that the function of commas is to help the reader to understand how the sentence is constructed. Can children identify where commas should have been used, and why?

Improving the writing

- **After the texts have been marked**: give the children time to read through your comments, to look at the success criteria and to implement any changes suggested. This should not involve the children rewriting the entire report – just those parts that you would like them to revisit to practise/improve their writing.

Share

Sometimes, children write text to practise writing text. Other times, there is a planned reason or an audience. If you want children to share their writing:

- let them rewrite and hand-illustrate their story and also word-process and find computer images for their non-fiction text; they can mount their texts opposite each other for display
- give them the opportunity to use their ideas in group or class debates
- let them plan marketing campaigns, supporting their point of view
- let them write a short text, explaining their feelings about writing the non-fiction and the fiction texts – they can then read aloud both their texts so a listener understands the contexts and the beliefs of the writer as they listen.

Unit 7: Writing a biased text and story with the same message

Name: **Class:** **Date:**

Make notes for the main points you will include in your biased text, and consider:
- how you will link paragraphs
- technical vocabulary you intend to use
- any other language features you think it would be useful to record.

	Fiction	Non-fiction
Point 1		
Point 2		
Point 3		
Summary statement		

Unit 7: Moderating writing: Writing a biased text and story with the same message

Name: Date:

	Contents	Text structure and organisation	Sentence structure	Vocabulary and descriptions	Punctuation	Spelling and handwriting
Working at greater depth within the expected standard	Cohesive links between paragraphs enable the reader to compare and contrast information given.	The level of formality in both texts is controlled and sometimes manipulated, to engage the reader.	Grammatical structures are manipulated to maintain the level of formality.	Vocabulary is manipulated to maintain the level of formality.	A full range of taught punctuation is used, mostly accurately.	Handwriting is effortlessly fast, fluent and easy to read.
	Topic sentences effectively introduce and summarise paragraphs.		Controlled and appropriate use of the passive voice is included where appropriate.	Technical and subject specific vocabulary used is integrated well into text.	Colons and/or semi-colons are used accurately.	Spelling – including of less familiar words – is generally accurate.
Working at the expected standard	In both texts, ideas are effectively grouped together in paragraphs and show clear progression (e.g. chronological in the story and topical in the non-fiction text).	Persuasive techniques such as use of emotive language and choice of information create effective non-fiction text.	Determiners, pronouns, adverbials and prepositional phrases are used appropriately to aid cohesion between sentences and paragraphs.	Vocabulary is generally appropriate to the level of formality within the text.	Some parentheses are marked with commas, brackets or dashes.	Most words on the Year 5/6 list – or words of equivalent challenge – are correctly spelled.
			Verb tenses are consistently accurate and appropriate in both texts.		Commas are used in parentheses, before a non-finite clause and to separate clauses as well as in lists and after fronted adverbials.	Unstressed vowels are generally accurate.
	Dialogue is integrated and used (at least once) to advance action in the story.	Atmosphere, characters and setting are developed effectively in the story.	A wide range of clause structures is used, sometimes varying their position within the sentence.	Technical and subject specific vocabulary is used appropriately.	Largely correct use of inverted commas and associated punctuation is shown.	Legibility, fluency and speed determine which letters are left unjoined.
			At least one appropriate use of the passive voice is included.		Some use of colons or semi-colons is included.	Handwriting is easily legible and may be sloped forwards for speed.
Working towards the expected standard	Paragraphs are generally used to organise ideas.	Some persuasive features are used.	Some pronouns and adverbials are used to aid cohesion between paragraphs.	There is evidence of some technical and subject specific vocabulary being used.	Apostrophes are consistently used correctly.	Some words on the Year 5/6 list – or words of equivalent challenge – are correctly spelled.
	Events are told in a coherent sequence.		Fronted adverbials at the beginning of paragraphs indicate a change of time		Commas are used within a series of actions to clarify meaning.	In handwriting, most letters are appropriately joined.

Where Should Sports Funding Be Aimed?

From one gold to 27 golds in 20 years
At the end of the Atlanta Olympics in 1996, Great Britain was 36th in the medal table, winning one gold in a rowing competition, together with eight silver and six bronze medals; 20 years later, in Rio in 2016, Team GB came second in the medals table, winning 27 gold, 23 silver and 17 bronze medals.

£80 million a year for UK Sport
What changed? The answer is the National Lottery. After the Atlanta Olympics, UK Parliament allowed for National Lottery "good causes" to give money to an organisation called UK Sport to support Olympic and Paralympic athletes. By 2016, the lottery proudly supported UK Sport to the tune of over £80 million a year. Being a world-class professional athlete is an expensive business. There are the costs of equipment and training facilities, coaches, performance gear, physiotherapists, dieticians, psychologists, doctors, masseurs and a myriad of other people whose support is critical if an Olympic or Paralympic athlete is to be at the top of their game during the four-yearly Olympics or Paralympics cycle.

Olympic Gold Medals Rio 2016	
Athletics	2
Boxing	1
Canoeing	2
Cycling	6
Diving	1
Equestrian	2
Golf	1
Gymnastics	2
Hockey	1
Rowing	3
Sailing	2
Swimming	1
Taekwondo	1
Tennis	1
Triathlon	1

Funding for athletes in elite Olympic sports
UK Sport's key objective is to identify and support athletes who have a realistic chance of winning a medal within the next eight years. Promising athletes are identified early and it is often recommended that they join "elite sports" such as rowing, sailing, cycling, swimming, athletics and gymnastics, or the Paralympic equivalent. Each gold medal represents a total investment of about £4 million. Other Olympic and Paralympic sports such as weight-lifting, archery, badminton, basketball and rugby are comparatively low-funded because Team GB is not thought likely to win medals in these sports within the next two Olympics.

Olympic rings

Funding for grassroots participation

Notwithstanding that the £80 million a year allows a few talented athletes to win medals, an alternative approach would be to invest the money into schools, local sports clubs and good regional sports facilities. In 2016, the UK boasted just five indoor velodromes for cycling and ten Olympic-sized swimming pools. Instead of concentrating all our investment in a few places where the top athletes can train, should we be investing money into increasing the number of good facilities across the country?

	Olympic-sized swimming pool	Velodrome
Aberdeen	✓	
Bangor, County Down	✓	
Bristol	✓	
Cardiff	✓	
Derby		✓
Glasgow	✓	✓
Leeds	✓	
London	✓	✓
Manchester		✓
Newport		✓
Plymouth	✓	
Sheffield	✓	
Sunderland	✓	

Although only around 7 % of all children in the UK are educated in private schools, over 30 % of GB Olympic medallists since 2012 were privately educated. Of course, it may be that this is entirely due to the athletic talent of this group of children, but it would appear more likely that they had access to better coaches, facilities and equipment.

All Olympians started somewhere and most were talent-spotted by a local coach. Thus, the funding available to grassroots sports clubs is largely concentrated on football and the Olympic elite sports; rugby, cricket, tennis and judo (non-elite sports) all had their funding cut after the 2012 Olympics.

The UK is currently experiencing childhood obesity in 20 % of all children, and it has been shown that children now are generally less active and are less likely to be involved in sports than those 10 years ago. This is probably partly due to the lure of electronic media, but how many more children would be involved in sports if better facilities and training were more widely available and if the cost of participating in a sport was more affordable?

Elite sports or grassroots participation?

Even lottery funding has its limits. As a country, we can't afford to pump money into grassroots participation as well as into elite sports and Olympic glory. Which is more important? Our top athletes are now known, respected and winning on the world stage. On the one hand, after a successful Olympic games, there is a country-wide "feel-good factor" and more people sign up to sports and athletics clubs – but on the other hand, the evidence is that many soon drop out. What do you think? Would £80 million a year of grassroots investment into equipment, sports coaches and facilities transform sporting participation for you, or are you more likely to get involved in sports having seen successful Olympic athletes?

Unit 8: Where Should Sports Funding Be Aimed?

Name:　　　　　　　　　　　　　　Class:　　　　Date:

1. What is the main reason that GB did so much better in the 2016 Olympics than it had in 1996?

   _____

2. If you were head of UK Sport, would you look at the 2016 Olympic medals table and think that you had correctly identified the elite sports?

   Use information from the text to support your answer.

   _____

   _____

3. Why are basketball and wheelchair basketball not well funded?

   _____

4. According to the text, why are privately educated children more likely to win Olympic medals?

   _____

5. *"This is partly due to the lure of electronic media"*

   In this sentence, tick **one** word that *lure* is closest to in meaning.

   temptation ☐　　　　investment ☐

   bait ☐　　　　　　　trap ☐

6. Using information from the text, tick **one** box in each row to show whether each statement is a fact or an opinion.

	Fact	Opinion
It is expensive being a top athlete.		
It is good that UK Sport concentrates funding on elite sports.		
There are enough Olympic-sized swimming pools in the UK.		
We need to get more children participating in sports.		

Cracking Writing Year 6 · Unit 8

Unit 8 Writing a discussion

In this unit children will:
- read a discussion text, considering the function of the headings as signposts of key ideas
- explore the use of cohesive devices, adverbials, prepositions and conjunctions in balancing opinions
- identify features of formal language and consider its impact
- plan, draft, edit and improve a balanced discussion.

Stage 1: Responding to the text

Activities:

- Show children an image of the Olympic rings and ask them to draw the rings on large paper.
- In groups, ask children to note down in each ring:
  - what they know about where/when the games are held
  - what they know about the history of the Olympics
  - any sports or athletics events they associate with the Olympics
  - what they know about medals
  - any Team GB Olympians/Paralympians they have heard of.
- Ask groups to share what they know with the class.
- Before you read the text together, explain that it is a discussion text, which asks a question and gives information but which allows the reader to reach their own conclusion.
- Ensure the children understand the more technical language used in the text, e.g. *"physiotherapists"*, *"dieticians"*, *"psychologists"*, *"masseurs"*, *"myriad"*, *"elite"*, *"grassroots"*, *"participation"*, *"notwithstanding"*, as well as idioms such as *"to the tune of"* and *"pump money into"*. Tell the children the meaning of any new vocabulary.
- Read the text together and discuss what the children learnt that they could add to the information in the rings.
- Ask the children to answer the reading comprehension questions to ensure close reading of the text and good understanding.
- Together, share answers to the questions and discuss the strategies children used to answer them.

Resources needed:

Shared copy of the text (PDF/IWB/visualiser)
Image of the Olympic rings
Each group needs:
- large paper and marker pens

Each child needs:
- a copy of the text
- a copy of the comprehension questions.

Stage 2: Analysing the text structure and organisation

Activities:

- Ask children to read the text aloud to a response partner to revisit the text, develop fluency, ensure appropriate pronunciation of all words and to practise reading with good intonation and expression.
- Ask children to underline any new words or phrases. Take feedback and explain what these mean in context.

Summarising sections

- Discuss the headings. Do children think they are useful?

Resources needed:

Shared copy of the text (PDF/IWB/visualiser)
Image of the Olympic rings
Large paper
Each pair needs:
- sticky notes

Each child needs:
- a copy of the text
- different coloured highlighters/pens/pencils.

Ask them to *think, pair, share:*
- What is their function? (*To show how the ideas move through the text.*)
- Why is there not a heading for each paragraph? (*Some sequences of paragraphs are on the same subject, so can be grouped together.*)
- Are the headings useful summaries of each section? Could children suggest better headings?

- Model writing notes to record the key information in the first paragraph. Use your notes to write a 20–30 word summary of the paragraph. Highlight how you make your choices to ensure the summary is concise, written in sentences but still makes sense.
- Ask pairs of children to:
  - note down the key information in each of the five sections of the text
  - use their notes to create a summary of each section, which should be 20–30 words long (summaries should be written on sticky notes).

Analysing paragraphs

- Ask children to underline the topic sentence (first sentence) in each paragraph.
  - Tell them to circle the topic sentences that are questions. Discuss whether these sentences function differently from other topic sentences. What is the purpose of these questions?
- Ask children what they understand by the term 'cohesion' when discussing texts, e.g. *A text has cohesion if it is clear how the meanings of its parts fit together.* Cohesive devices that can help to do this include:
  - *determiners and pronouns* – which refer back to previous words
  - *conjunctions, prepositional phrases and adverbs* – which make relationships between ideas clear
  - *referral to things previously mentioned.*
- Work with children to identify examples of each cohesive device as a class before they work in their groups.
- Ask pairs of children to highlight/list cohesive devices (determiners, pronouns, adverbials, prepositional phrases, conjunctions) used to make links between the paragraphs.
- Let them share their lists with another pair to confirm they are identifying the same cohesive devices.

Stage 3: Analysing the text purpose and language

Activities:

Evaluating text for achieving its purpose

- Ask pairs of children to read the text aloud to each other and:
  - consider whether the author is trying to:
    - simply give information
    - persuade the reader to agree with their opinions
    - present different sides of an argument to help the reader to make up their own mind (*this is the intention*).
  - discuss *how* they know the answer, considering:
    - the title
    - the final, summary, section
    - organisation – different sections focus primarily on different ideas
    - use of questions
    - presentation mostly of facts rather than opinions.
- *Think, pair, share:* Give the children the opportunity to evaluate the effectiveness of the text in achieving its purpose.
  - The different sections of a text like this will show bias such as in the use of emotive language, e.g. *"pump money into; "boasted just ten Olympic-sized pools"; "lure of electronic media".* Do children think that, overall, the text is balanced or that the bias of the writer is clear?

Resources needed:

Shared copy of the text (PDF/IWB/visualiser)

Each child needs:
- a copy of the text
- coloured highlighters/pens/pencils.

- o How could the text be improved to become more balanced?
- o Ask children to annotate/mark/edit the text to show how and where improvements could be made and what these might be.

Exploring adverbials, prepositions and conjunctions

- Remind children of the role of:
  - o adverbials (*a word or phrase that is used to modify a verb or clause – adverbs, prepositional phrases and subordinate clauses can all be used in this way*)
  - o prepositional phrases (*begin with a preposition followed by a pronoun, noun or determiner*)
  - o conjunctions (*link two words, phrases or clauses together*).
- Model identifying examples of each word class.
- Explain to the children that there are some adverbs, prepositions and conjunctions that are particularly useful in discussion texts. Can they scan the text, find and underline:
  - o the adverbials ("*Notwithstanding*"; "*of course*"; "*more likely*"; "*thus*")
  - o prepositions ("*instead of*"; "*on the one hand … but on the other*")
  - o conjunctions ("*although*", "*but*")?
- Discuss why these words are mostly found in the second half of the text (*because the other side of the argument is introduced*).
- Talk about the impact of this language on clarifying the purpose of the text.

Analysing formality

- All texts are written using a range of language in order that the texts are not too 'samey' and boring to read.
- Ask children to consider whether this text is primarily written:
  - o in the first person (look for pronouns *I, me, we, us, mine, ours*)
  - o in the second person (look for pronouns *you, yours*)
  - o in the third person (look for pronouns *he, she, they, them, theirs*).
- Agree that it's mostly in the third person but with questions directed at the reader (second person).
  - o Discuss the impact of this decision. How would the text change if there were no second person sentences?
- Ask children whether they think the language of the text is formal or informal. Model identifying some examples of formal and informal language before asking children to use agreed colours to identify examples of formal/informal language such as:

Formal language	Informal language
Less speech-like sentence types such as:	Contractions (*can't*)
- passives (e.g. "*Promising athletes are identified*"; "*it has been shown*")	Idioms ("*an expensive business*"; "*pump money*")
- conditionals ("*It may be that*")	General verb (*get*) rather than specific verb (*become*)
- subjunctive ("*it is often recommended that they join*")	Second person pronouns (*you*)
Longer sentences with more clauses	Incomplete sentences
More advanced punctuation (e.g. semi-colons, dashes, hyphens)	Adverbs such as *anyway*
Vocabulary you might hear on news programmes and documentaries (*participating* rather than *joining in*; *currently* rather than *now*) – link to language explored at Stage 1	Sentences may start with conjunctions, e.g. *and, but, so, because*
Generally written in the third person	
Specialist adverbials (e.g. "*Notwithstanding*", "*of course*"), conjunctions (e.g. *although*) and prepositions (e.g. *the one hand*)	

- Use examples from the text to discuss the impact on the reader of the level of formality of this text.
  - Does it have more formal or informal features? Why?
  - How would increasing the informality change the impact of the text?
  - Talk about why the author may have chosen this level of formality, but included some informal features too.

Analysing punctuation

- What can children tell you about the function of semi-colons (*mark a boundary between two closely related independent clauses*), parentheses (*additional information not constrained by the grammar of the main clause*) and ellipses (*a way of indicating pauses*)?
- In pairs, ask children to highlight and identify uses of:
  - semi-colons (e.g. *"winning one gold in a rowing competition, together with eight silver and six bronze medals; 20 years later"*)
  - dashes (*"more people sign up to sports and athletics clubs – but the evidence so far is that many soon drop out"*)
  - hyphens (e.g. *"world-class professional"; "talent-spotted"; "country-wide"; "feel-good factor"*)
  - parentheses (*"20 years later, in Rio in 2016, Team GB"*).
- For each, discuss the impact of the punctuation and what other grammatical choices the author might have had.

Stage 4: Planning to write: Writing a discussion

Activities:

- Prior to the session, identify the topic you would like children to write about. Look for a topic that is familiar and motivating to the children, and for which they should be able to list ideas supporting both sides. Ideally, make some link to current curriculum or social issues in class, but other ideas could include:
  - Is it better to borrow money from your parents/carers to buy something, or to save up for it?
  - Should you say what you would like for a gift or enjoy the surprise when it comes?
  - Is it more interesting to read a book or to watch a film?

  You may want to amend the success criteria (online at My Rising Stars) to reflect the topics.
- Tell the children that they are going to write a discussion text, based on the model text, about the subject you have chosen.
- Revisit the organisation of the ideas in the model text:
  - Clarify that in this discussion, the writer chose to separate out the arguments in the text.
  - Discuss alternative ways of presenting ideas in a discussion paper, for example balancing the pros and cons of each idea in the same paragraph.
- In groups, ask children to discuss the questions under consideration between them, finding as many reasons for both sides of the discussion as they can. Ask children to record their ideas on sticky notes, using a different note for each idea and a different colour for each side of the discussion.
- Borrow some sticky notes from different groups until you have a range of ideas. Model your thoughts as a writer as you try to make decisions about how to organise the ideas: in sections, as in the model text, or one point immediately balanced by a counter-argument.
- Give children time to explore moving their sticky notes around to decide how they think their text should be organised.

Resources needed:

Shared copy of the text (PDF/IWB/visualiser)

The success criteria

Each group needs:
- two different colours of sticky notes

Each child needs:
- the copy of the text they have previously highlighted and annotated
- the writing framework from page 93 (some children may benefit from this being enlarged to A3) or success criteria if a different writing framework is used
- different coloured pens/pencils.

Cracking Writing Year 6 · Unit 8

- Take feedback from different groups about how they have decided to organise their ideas – and why this approach is recommended.
- Introduce the writing framework. Think of a question that encapsulates the discussion and use that as your title. Model completing the writing framework, based on the ideas you organised previously and using concise notes to capture the main ideas you want to present on either side of the discussion. Use the boxes at the foot of the framework to note down ideas for headings and also to capture the specialist adverbials, prepositional phrases and conjunctions that help to create a discussion text.
- Ask children to work in pairs with the writing framework. Ask children to:
  - complete the writing framework, identifying two or three ideas from each side of the argument to include
  - use colour to number the order in which they plan to make their points
  - suggest headings they might use
  - record some useful specialist adverbials, conjunctions and prepositional phrases.
- Briefly, revisit the model text to look at the comparative points about:
  - ways ideas are linked
  - text organisation and structure of paragraphs
  - paragraph openings
  - language, tense, pronouns, punctuation, sentence beginnings.
- Ask children to swap partners so they can talk through their ideas with new partners.
  - In addition to sharing the notes, children should try talking through some of the ideas in more depth with this new talk partner.
  - Encourage them to annotate the paper with additional ideas, information, vocabulary and phrases. They can also include notes about feedback and suggestions given.
- Give children time to make improvements based on feedback from response partners.
- Ask the children to suggest success criteria for a discursive text. Use their ideas to clarify and edit the success criteria (online at My Rising Stars).

Stage 5: Writing

Activities:

- Remind children that their task is to write a discussion text on the topic you have given them. They should aim to present both sides of the argument.
- Model writing an opening paragraph, following the plan you created at Stage 4 (above). In your paragraph, demonstrate the use of more formal language, including some of the specialist adverbials, prepositional phrases and conjunctions previously identified. Try to include at least one instance of the passive voice to hide the agent when it isn't important and use commas to mark parentheses.
- Before they start, give children a few minutes to 'talk like a writer' and tell their partner the text as they plan to write it. If it helps, ask them to use a polite 'writer's voice'.
- Let response partners give some brief feedback before children swap roles.
- Read aloud the success criteria (online at My Rising Stars).
- Let the children write.
- Throughout the writing session, quietly let the children know how long they have spent, where in their text they should expect to be now and how long there is left.
- Five minutes before the end of the session, ask all children to stop writing and read their text aloud to themselves. If they find errors, missing words or words they can improve, they should use this opportunity to make changes.

Resources needed:

Each child needs:
- the copy of the text they have previously annotated
- the completed and annotated writing framework, including the success criteria.

Cracking Writing Year 6 · Unit 8

Stage 6: Improving, editing, reviewing and sharing the writing

Activities:

- Revisit together the success criteria (online at My Rising Stars).
- Model the process below using your work as an example. The children can give you feedback on each step of the process. After you model a step, the children should have a go with their partner at editing their own work.

Resources needed:

Each child needs:
- the success criteria
- their writing/completed writing framework
- different coloured highlighters/pens.

- Ask children to reread their texts three times with their response partner:
  - First read through: Children read their partner's text out loud to them. The child who wrote the text listens to check that their writing makes sense, listens out for obvious errors and checks the text follows their plan. Children then swap roles.
  - Second read through: Children read their partner's text and highlight the success criteria they have met. They suggest three places where their partner could improve their work (to achieve or further improve on the success criteria).
  - Third read through: Children proofread their partner's text together with them. They check for errors in punctuation and spelling and correct these as necessary. You should give input at this stage if needed.

Lessons from writing

- Prior to the session, identify errors that were commonly made. Write sample sentences that need to be corrected and ask the children to help you to fix them. These could include:
  - not using the passive, e.g.
    - Some people argue that if someone doesn't pick up their things, then they shouldn't get their pocket money. I disagree because as long as things someone picks up everything, does it matter who does it?
    - There are two opportunities to use the passive in this text. Can children spot them, change them to the passive and then indicate whether or not they think the text is improved?
  - language is too informal and too biased, e.g.
    - Why do people say they'd rather watch a film? I just don't get it. When you read a book, you've got all the time you want to read a bit at the speed you want to read. And you get to know what the characters are thinking as well as what they do. It's so much better.
    - Challenge children to recreate a text like this in a more formal style and with less obvious bias.

Improving the writing

- **After the texts have been marked:** give the children time to read through your comments, to look at the success criteria and to implement any changes suggested. This should not involve the children rewriting the entire text – just those parts that you would like them to revisit to practise/improve their writing.

Share

Sometimes, children write text to practise writing text. Other times, there is a planned reason or an audience. If you want children to share their writing:

- make an interactive display: give children different coloured speech bubbles to write separate points from their text; display the speech bubbles on either side of a list of useful adverbials, conjunctions and prepositional phrases; provide strands of thick wool and drawing pins/sticky tack so that children can select phrases to join/oppose the ideas in the speech bubbles
- organise group debates where they have to argue one side or the other; ask 'reporters' for each debate to word-process a brief article about the points raised and publish their writing in a magazine format
- depending on the topic, it may be appropriate for them to reframe their ideas into letters which present balanced ideas but with a slight bias for one approach or the other.

Cracking Writing Year 6 © Rising Stars UK Ltd 2017.

Unit 8: Writing a discussion

Name: Class: Date:

Question as title: _____

How will you organise the ideas in your discussion?

Make notes to capture the main ideas for each side of your discussion below.

What headings will you use?

Note down any adverbials, prepositional phrases or conjunctions that are good to use in a discussion text.

Unit 8: Moderating writing: Writing a discussion

Name: Date:

	Contents	Text structure and organisation	Sentence structure	Vocabulary and descriptions	Punctuation	Spelling and handwriting
Working at greater depth within the expected standard	The level of formality of different parts of the text is reflected in paragraph structure.	A subtle bias is introduced through the structure and organisation of ideas.	Grammatical structures are manipulated to maintain/change the level of formality.	Vocabulary is manipulated to maintain/change the level of formality.	A full range of taught punctuation is used, mostly accurately.	Handwriting is effortlessly fast, fluent and easy to read.
	Topic sentences effectively introduce and summarise paragraphs.		The passive voice is used to create a sense of authority and formality.		Colons and/or semi-colons are used accurately.	Spelling – including of less familiar words – is generally accurate.
Working at the expected standard	Paragraphs are used effectively to progress the sequence of ideas through the text.	Ideas are well organised and presented coherently to create an unbiased discussion.	Determiners, pronouns, adverbials and prepositional phrases are used appropriately to aid cohesion between sentences and paragraphs.	Vocabulary is generally appropriate to the level of formality within the text.	Some parentheses are marked with commas, brackets or dashes.	Most words on the Year 5/6 list – or words of equivalent challenge – are correctly spelled.
					Commas are used in lists, separating clauses, following fronted adverbials, parentheses, before a non-finite (-ing) clause.	Unstressed vowels are generally accurate.
	Headings are used appropriately to continue the style of the model text.		At least one appropriate use of passive voice to disguise/hide agent is included.	Adverbs and prepositional phrases add detail and precision.	Some use of colons or semi-colons is included.	Legibility, fluency and speed determine which letters are left unjoined.
						Handwriting is easily legible and may be sloped forwards for speed.
Working towards the expected standard	Paragraphs are generally used to organise ideas.	The overall purpose of the text is evident in the balance of ideas included.	Pronouns and adverbials are used to aid cohesion.	Some relevant specialist vocabulary is used.	Apostrophes are consistently used correctly.	Some words on the Year 5/6 list – or words of equivalent challenge – are correctly spelled.
			Fronted adverbials at the beginning of paragraphs indicate a when, where or how ideas are relevant.		Commas are used within a series of actions to clarify meaning.	In handwriting, most letters are appropriately joined.

Cracking Writing Year 6 © Rising Stars UK Ltd 2017. You may photocopy this page.

What is the World?

James Carter

A scientist may say:
"70% water, 30% land."

A geologist may say:
"4.6 billion years old."

An astronomer may say:
"The merest speck
on a cosmic coast
awash on the tide of time."

A myth maker may say:
"A glorious orb
held aloft
by elephants
atop a giant turtle."

A priest may say:
"A miracle."

An astronaut may say:
"Home."

An ecologist may say:
"Poorly."

Unit 9: What is the World?

Name: Class: Date:

1. What is 4.6 billion years old?

   _____

2. *"The merest speck on a cosmic coast"*

   In this phrase, tick **one** word that *merest* is closest to in meaning.

   most comfortable ☐   most beautiful ☐

   most insignificant ☐   most admired ☐

3. Why is the myth maker more likely to talk about turtles and elephants than the priest?

   _____

4. Where do you think an astronaut would be when he said *"Home"*?

   _____

5. Why would an ecologist describe the planet as *"Poorly"*?

   _____

6. Tick **one** box in each line to indicate whether each of the people in the poem is offering facts or opinions.

	Fact	Opinion
Scientist		
Geologist		
Astronomer		
Myth maker		
Priest		
Astronaut		
Ecologist		

Cracking Writing Year 6 · Unit 9

Unit 9 Writing free verse

In this unit children will:
- read a poem written in free verse and consider its organisation of ideas
- identify the poem's mood and consider how this is conveyed
- evaluate features of the poem and its structure
- consider language use and punctuation
- plan, draft, edit and improve new sections for a poem, considering where to insert them.

Stage 1: Responding to the text

Activities:

- Share prior knowledge of Planet Earth.
- Ask pairs to make their own mind map of Planet Earth facts. These could include:
  - where it is in relation to other planets
  - the position and significance of the equator, Tropics of cancer and Capricorn, Greenwich meridian, etc.
  - how many continents there are (as well as major countries and cities on each continent)
  - information about physical geography (including curriculum information about biomes, rivers, mountains, volcanoes and earthquakes)
  - habitats and the creatures that live in them (including jungles, deserts, grasslands, tundra and coasts)
  - information about human geography (including curriculum information about distribution of energy, food, minerals and water)
  - ecological information about the climate, impact of cutting down rainforest, etc.
- Use children's ideas to make a class mind map about Planet Earth.
- Before you read the text together, ensure the children understand the more technical/ambitious language used in the text, e.g. *"geologist"*, *"astronomer"*, *"myth maker"*, *"ecologist"*, *"speck"*, *"cosmic"*, *"orb"* and *"aloft"*. Tell the children the meaning of any new vocabulary.
- Introduce the poet James Carter, who lives and works in Oxfordshire.
- Read the poem together and discuss:
  - Why do all these people describe the World in different ways? They're talking about the same thing!
  - Was there anything from their list that was also in the poem?
  - What did they learn from the poem?
- Ask the children to answer the reading comprehension questions to ensure close reading of the poems and good understanding.
- Together, share answers to the questions and discuss the strategies children used to answer them.

Resources needed:

Shared copy of the text (PDF/IWB/visualiser)

Each group needs:
- large paper and marker pens

Each child needs:
- a copy of the text
- a copy of the comprehension questions.

Stage 2: Analysing the poem's content

Activities:

- Ask children to read the poem aloud to a response partner in order to revisit the text, develop fluency, ensure accurate pronunciation of all words and to practise reading with expression and a reasonable speaking pace.
- Ask children to underline any new words or phrases. Take feedback and explain what these mean in context.

Discussing idea development

- In pairs, ask children to cut up the poem so that each of the people and what they say is on a separate strip of paper. Suggest that they number the strips so they know their original order.
- Demonstrate reorganising the strips of paper to create a different version of the same poem. Read it aloud to the children and talk about its impact:
  - Is there any strip of paper that has to go first or last?
  - Does it matter in which order the other strips are?
- As children answer, ask them to explain their thinking. Encourage them to think about:
  - the pattern made by the length of the speeches at different parts of the poem
  - whether they think there is a relationship between each successive speaker
  - the type of information given by the speakers and how it changes through the poem.
- In pairs, ask children to reorganise the strips of paper to create new versions of the poem. Each time they settle on a new order, they should read the poem aloud and see whether it 'works'. When they create a successful poem, tell them to make a note of the order of the strips (using the number noted earlier).
- Let pairs read their successful reordered poem to another pair and together discuss the impact of the new order. If both pairs think a reordered poem is good, allow them to read their poems to another group of four.
- Allow groups of eight to read their best reordered poem aloud to the rest of the class and explain why the order they agreed on is successful.
- Compare each newly ordered poem to the original and decide each time which is better and why. Each time, remind children to consider the three questions above (pattern of length of speeches; relationship between speeches; information given in speeches).

Discussing mood

- Together, discuss the mood of the poem.
  - Is the topic serious or light-hearted?
  - Is the language formal or informal?
  - How much description is there?
  - Accept other ideas the children share, with evidence.
- Ask children to suggest what the poet might have been trying to achieve with this poem; what does he want the reader to think at the end? Is there a 'message'? Ask them to give evidence for each answer.
- Why are the myth maker and astronomer the ones who use descriptive language, rather than the scientists? (*Because the scientists use precise, scientific language, whereas astronomers and myth makers are more creative in their interpretations.*)

Resources needed:

Shared copy of the text (PDF/IWB/visualiser)

Each pair needs:
- scissors
- an additional copy of the text

Each child needs:
- their own copy of the text
- additional paper for making notes.

Cracking Writing Year 6 · Unit 9

Stage 3: Analysing the language

Activities:

Evaluating the structure

- Reread the poem aloud to the children and ask them to consider:
    - Does it rhyme? (*No.*)
    - Does it have a regular rhythm? (*No.*)
    - Does it have a regular beat? (*No.*)
    - Is there any clear pattern to the lines? (*Each new segment starts with "A [professional] may say".*)
- *Think, pair, share:* What makes this text a poem? How is it different from a fiction or non-fiction text?
- Together, explore some ideas about poems and see if they fit this one:
    - language use is precise and concise
    - figurative language and idiom can express ideas neatly
    - each line expresses an idea or a phrase
    - the whole poem reflects the writer's wish to make sense of something and to share their understanding with others
    - interpretation can be left to the reader so different people can read different messages into it
    - writing doesn't have to be in sentences or to have punctuation – though it can.

Analysing language

- In pairs, ask children to consider:
    - whether the poem is written in sentences (*yes – because of the verb "may" in the lines "A [professional] may say" but the speeches are phrases, not sentences*)
    - whether the language is descriptive (*yes – the astronomer and myth maker use adjectives and precise nouns; the scientists and the geologist use appropriate language which is specific and exact*)
    - synonyms for "*poorly*" in the final line (e.g. *unwell, sick, ailing, ill*) – talk about why the poet might have chosen "*poorly*" instead of any other synonym.

Analysing punctuation

- Ask children to scan the poem, highlighting all punctuation marks they see.
- *Think, pair, share:* How is punctuation used? E.g.
    - Colons are used between the name of the speaker and what they say. Clarify that this is a legitimate use of colons, though less likely to be used in stories.
    - Inverted commas show the beginning and end of speech.
    - A full stop marks the end of each speech and section. Capital letters are used at the beginning of each section (e.g. "*A scientist*") and at the beginning of each speech. Unlike many poems, this one doesn't have a capital at the beginning of each line.
    - The only comma is in the list in "*70% water, 30% land*".
- Ask children why they think the poet used punctuation when it's not necessary in poetry. Clarify that writers need to know that their readers understand their text and that the role of the punctuation is always to clarify meaning.

Resources needed:

Shared copy of the text (PDF/IWB/visualiser)

Each group needs:
- an enlarged A3 copy of the poem

Each child needs:
- a copy of the text
- highlighters/pens/pencils.

Cracking Writing Year 6 · Unit 9

Stage 4: Planning to write: Writing free verse

Activities:

- Tell the children that you would like them to add new sections into the poem about the world.
- In groups ask children to list different people who might have a view of the world (e.g. *a baby, a zoologist, a teacher, a cleaner, a doctor, a lawyer, an Imam, a soldier, a refugee, a policeman, a sailor, a poet*).
- Model creating a new part to the poem based on one of the people children suggest, e.g.

    A baby may say:
    "Ball";
    A zoologist may say:
    "Diverse habitats
    allow for an abundance of wildlife."

    o Ask children to give you feedback and ideas as you work.
    o Comment on your own thought processes.
- In their groups, ask pairs of children to use the strips of paper to link a person to a thought about the world. Encourage children to use their mind map for ideas about the world and a thesaurus to help them with their selection of precise and concise words.
- As a group, ask children to mix some of their favourite sections of the original poem with new sections they have created.

    o Let groups share their new poems with others.
- Distribute the writing framework.

    o Explain that the words at the bottom are there to remind children of the range of ideas they could use in their poem. They are not confined to these ideas.
    o Model how you would record some new ideas into the writing framework (e.g. *An astronomer may say: In orbit/around a far-off star./A refugee may say: 'Dangerous/and unwelcoming.'*)
- Let children work individually or in pairs to record at least eight ideas on their writing framework.
- Ask children to work with a response partner so they can talk through and improve their ideas.
- Give children time to make improvements based on feedback from response partners.
- Ask the children to suggest success criteria for adding a new section to the poem. Use their ideas to edit the success criteria (online at My Rising Stars).

Resources needed:

Shared copy of the text (PDF/IWB/visualiser)

The success criteria:

Each group needs:
- the strips of poem they had at Stage 2
- strips of paper
- thesauruses

Each child needs:
- the copy of the text they have previously highlighted and annotated
- the mind map they made during Stage 1
- the writing framework from page 102 (some children may benefit from this being enlarged to A3) or success criteria if a different writing framework is used.

Stage 5: Writing

Activities:

- Remind children that you want them to write some new sections into the poem about the World.
- If possible, use IT as you model using the ideas you planned at Stage 4, polishing them with the aid of a thesaurus. With children's help, ensure that you use precise nouns and concise noun phrases.

Resources needed:

The success criteria

Each child needs:
- the copy of the poem they have previously annotated
- the completed and annotated writing framework, including the success criteria
- a PC/laptop/tablet if the children are word-processing.

Cracking Writing Year 6 · Unit 9

- Before they start to create their own poem, give children a few minutes to 'talk like a writer' and tell their partner some of the sections as they plan to write them. If it helps, ask them to use a polite 'writer's voice'.
- Let response partners give some brief feedback before children swap roles.
- Read aloud the success criteria (online at My Rising Stars).
- If children are using IT, remind them that they can jot down any ideas and then edit and amend as they write.
- Let the children write. Remind them that if they are using IT, they can easily change the order of their sections to ensure a good balance of ideas and patterns running though their new poem.
- Throughout the writing session, quietly let the children know how long they have spent, where in their text they should expect to be now and how long there is left.
- Five minutes before the end of the session, ask all children to stop writing and read their text aloud to themselves. If they find errors, or missing words or words they can improve, they should use this opportunity to make changes.

Stage 6: Improving, editing, reviewing and sharing the writing

Activities:

- Revisit together the success criteria (online at My Rising Stars).
- Model the process below using your work as an example. The children can give you feedback on each step of the process. After you model a step the children should have a go with their partner at editing their own work.
- Ask children to reread their texts three times with their response partner:
  - First read through: Children read their partner's text out loud to them. The child who wrote the text listens to check that their writing makes sense, listens out for obvious errors and checks the text follows their plan. Children then swap roles.
  - Second read through: Children read their partner's text and highlight the success criteria they have met. They suggest three places where their partner could improve their work (to achieve or further improve on the success criteria).
  - Third read through: Children proofread their partner's text together with them. They check for errors in punctuation and spelling and correct these as necessary. You should give input at this stage if needed.

Resources needed:

Each child needs:
- the success criteria
- their writing/completed writing framework
- different coloured highlighters/pens.

Lessons from writing

- Prior to the session, identify errors that were commonly made. Write sample sentences that need to be corrected and ask the children to help you to fix them. These could include:
  - imprecise adjectives, e.g. *A happy person may say: A lovely blue sky*.
    - How many different ways can they improve that phrase? Can they add in a prepositional phrase as well?
  - all noun phrases extended with an adjective, e.g. *An exploding mountain;*
    - Explore how these can be varied, improved and extended using prepositional phrases.

Improving the writing

- **After the texts have been marked**: give the children time to read through your comments, to look at the success criteria and to implement any changes suggested. This should not involve the children rewriting the entire text – just those parts that you would like them to revisit to practise/improve their writing.

Share

Sometimes, children write text to practise writing text. Other times, there is a planned reason or an audience. If you want children to share their writing:

- poems are often ideal for performance – give children the opportunity to read, rehearse and continue to improve their poems before they perform to another class, in an assembly or on video for the class website.
- print out poems and allow children to illustrate them to make a class poetry book.

Unit 9: Writing free verse

Name:　　　　　　　　　　　　　　　　　　　　Class:　　　　Date:

Record some ideas for what different people may say about the world. Use the words at the bottom for ideas.

A _____ may say:	Record some ideas, here. Edit and improve them as you go.	Order your ideas.

- Landscape (e.g. *mountains, hills, rivers*)
- Creatures
- Resources we need (e.g. *water, power, minerals*)
- Resources creatures need (e.g. *food, shelter*)
- Habitats (e.g. *rainforests, deserts, grasslands, coasts*)
- Looking after the planet
- Countries
- Volcanoes and earthquakes
- Where our food comes from
- Planet
- Solar system
- Stories
- Looking after each other

Unit 9: Moderating writing: Writing free verse

Name: Date:

	Contents	Text structure and organisation	Sentence structure	Vocabulary and descriptions	Punctuation	Spelling and handwriting
Working at greater depth within the expected standard	The combination of new and existing sections is well balanced and skilfully managed.	The nature of the speaker in each sentence determines the type of language used.	A balance of shorter and longer sentences is achieved.	Controlled and thoughtful word choice is used to create a consistent 'mood' throughout the poem.	Line breaks are used sensitively within longer phrases.	Spelling – including of less familiar words – is generally accurate.
				Careful choice of detail enables accurate, concise description.		Word-processing is fast, fluent and generally accurate.
Working at the expected standard	At least six new sections are interspersed between at least three carefully selected sections from the existing poem.	There is a flow of ideas through the revised poem.		Precise and concise vocabulary 'is used to say more with fewer words'.	Punctuation is based on the model text and includes colons, inverted commas, capital letters and full stops.	Most words on the Year 5/6 list – or words of equivalent challenge – are correctly spelled.
		All speeches are appropriate to the speakers in style and content.		Some noun phrases are expanded with prepositional phrases to create more descriptive and creative sentences.	All punctuation that is used is accurate.	Unstressed vowels are generally accurate.
						Word-processing is at least as fast as handwriting and often accurate.
Working towards the expected standard	The poem is based on the model and includes at least four new sections together with three from the existing poem.	The pattern of sentences from the model poem is successfully copied.	The poem includes a mixture of shorter and longer sentences.	Some appropriate and accurate vocabulary is used to help to interest the reader.	Most punctuation that is used is accurate.	Some words on the Year 5/6 list – or words of equivalent challenge – are correctly spelled.
						Word-processing is nearly as fast as handwriting.

Answers

> Cracking Writing Year 6

Unit 1
1. ✓ shyly
2. a badly skinned whale
3. Gerald — thinks it's old fashioned
   Larry — thinks it's a monstrosity
   Margo — scared of it
   Roger — amused but mystified by it
   (Gerald → thinks it's old fashioned; Larry → amused but mystified by it; Margo → thinks it's a monstrosity; Roger → scared of it)
4. Her children don't like her bathing costume.
5. It was Mother wearing her bathing costume.
6. The bathing costume is described as "an extraordinarily shapeless garment" and the children genuinely don't know what it's for at first. However, Mother had been persuaded by her children to get a bathing costume and the one she bought was "voluminous" and "rippling with frills" which would cover up the figure she had "when you get to my age".

Unit 2
1. Chickens had settled into their new roosts; didn't need to corral the pigs; they had lamp oil and nets for fishing.
2. Tam
3. Pa's back ached.
4.

Before, when they lived in a forest	Now they live near a hill
The family ate bush-meat.	They eat rats and fish.
Pa was the Bee man.	Pa was just a farmer, just a man.

5. No. they were forced to move; they had to eat rats; Tam couldn't go to lessons; Pa and Tam are having to work to clear the stones from their field; the land is very dry.
6. To emphasise the surprise/suddenness/devastating impact of the event.

Unit 3
1. The change between night and day was really fast.
2. ✓ It was made of marble.
   ✓ Its wings were spread out.
   ✓ It was like a sphinx.
3. He would be able to escape.
4. ✓ He is worried about what he will find.
5. ✓ experiences
6. Several examples including: "with it a certain dread"; "the full audacity of my voyage came suddenly upon me" and other examples in that paragraph; "I felt naked in a strange world".

Unit 4
1. He praised Macbeth and him warmly; he said he would visit Macbeth's castle.
2. ✓ fate
3. To kill King Duncan and the king's son and heir, Malcolm.
4. Similarity: Macbeth was ambitious; Lady Macbeth honoured power and ambition.
   Difference: Macbeth had a sense of honour; Lady Macbeth was quite ruthless.
5. She appeared sweet and charming to Duncan whilst plotting his murder.
6. Lady Macbeth is blamed more: she won't let Macbeth change his mind; she influences and persuades him; she drugs the guards. Macbeth does the deed but is immediately horrified by it whereas Lady Macbeth's evil heart "swelled with satisfaction".

Unit 5
1. The earliest art we know about was created for ritual purposes.
2. The Minoans traded with Egyptians.
3. ✓ nearly
4. They used observations of real life in their art.
5. Art was used for ritual purposes: Egyptians
   Artists painted pictures of animals: Egyptians *, Minoans, Mycenaeans*, Greeks
   The style was influenced by Ancient Egyptian art: Minoans, Mycenaeans
   Artwork tried to show what people and animals really looked like: Greeks
   Images were painted on walls or storage jars: Egyptians, Minoans, Mycenaeans* and Greeks.
   *Although the text doesn't state that these facts are true, children may know it from their own experience.
6. The information is shown chronologically/in time order/in sequence.

Unit 6
1. (a) bigmouth   (b) so called friend
   (c) real friend   (d) bully
2. You can talk to them and they don't try to take over.
3. You act less calmly; bottled up feelings often erupt.
4. It helps you get things out of your system; it helps you see what's going on more clearly; it helps you be happier and calmer too; it can also be used as evidence.
5. Notebooks allow you to write as much or as little as you like, and to draw pictures.

Cracking Writing Year 6

6.

Same	Different
You need a date.	You write in one and draw in the other.
You record how you feel.	In drawings, you don't have to draw what people really look like; if writing, you record facts.
You use some useful words to remind you of what happened.	

Unit 7
1. It is in the rainforest/there are berries/the river joins the Amazon (so it is in Brazil).
2. No, because the *nabë* take away every tree which means the animals die and the people starve. *or* Yes, because the *nabë* will take what they want anyway but if you help them, there are rewards.
3. The clearings made by the Yanomami people are small and the forest can recover; the *nabë* make huge clearings, taking away all the trees so the animals have no food and don't spread the seed which allows the forest to recover.
4. Because the timber workers are cutting down trees.
5. Forest plants and creatures could help to solve hunger and cure sick people; the rainforests control the planet's climate.
6.

	Fiction	Non-fiction
Rainforests are being cut down.	✓	✓
The Yanomami people can't live without the rainforest.	✓	
Some plants in the rainforests can be used to cure disease.	✓	✓
The rainforests help to control the Earth's climate.		✓
All the trees, plants, creatures and insects must be saved together – it's no use just saving some of them.	✓	✓

Unit 8
1. They had funding through the national lottery.
2. Most elite sports were correctly identified, but more medals were won in Equestrian and Canoeing than in swimming.
3. No medals were won or were expected to be won in either basketball or wheelchair basketball.
4. They have access to better coaches, facilities and equipment.
5. ✓ temptation
6.

	Fact	Opinion
It is expensive being a top athlete.	✓	
It is good that UK Sport concentrates funding on elite sports.		✓
There are enough Olympic sized swimming pools in the UK.		✓
We need to get more children participating in sports.		✓

Unit 9
1. The world/Planet Earth
2. ✓ most insignificant
3. Because myths try to explain how things are. No religion has the belief that the world is held by elephants on the back of a turtle.
4. in space
5. Climate change and pollution are making Earth unhealthy.
6.

	Fact	Opinion
Scientist	✓	
Geologist	✓	
Astronomer		✓
Myth maker		✓
Priest		✓
Astronaut	✓	
Ecologist	✓	

If children disagree with these ticks, ask them to justify their answers – some people's facts are other people's opinions.